Essentials in an Aimless World

STRENGTHENING *Your* GRIP

BIBLE STUDY GUIDE

From the Bible-teaching ministry of

Charles R. Swindoll

Insight for Living

Chuck graduated in 1963 from Dallas Theological Seminary, where he now serves as the school's fourth president, helping to prepare a new generation of men and women for the ministry. Chuck has served in pastorates in three states: Massachusetts, Texas, and California, including almost twenty-three years at the First Evangelical Free Church in Fullerton, California. His sermon messages have been aired over radio since 1979 as the *Insight for Living* broadcast. A best-selling author, Chuck has written numerous books and booklets on many subjects.

Based on the outlines and transcripts of Chuck's sermons, the study guide text is coauthored by Ken Gire and Gary Matlack. Ken is a graduate of Texas Christian University and Dallas Theological Seminary. Gary is a graduate of Texas Tech University and Dallas Theological Seminary. He also wrote the Living Insights sections.

Editor in Chief:
Cynthia Swindoll
Coauthors of Text:
Ken Gire
Gary Matlack
Author of Living Insights:
Gary Matlack
Assistant Editor:
Wendy Peterson
Copy Editors:
Tom Kimber
Glenda Schlahta
Karene Wells
Text Designer:
Gary Lett
Publishing System Specialist:
Bob Haskins
Cover Designer:
Nina Paris
Director, Communications and Marketing Division:
Deedee Snyder
Marketing Manager:
Alene Cooper
Project Coordinator:
Colette Muse
Production Manager:
John Norton
Printer:
Sinclair Printing Company

ISBN 0-8499-8643-5
COVER PHOTOGRAPH: Tony Stone Images
Printed in the United States of America

CONTENTS

INTRODUCTION

A firm grip is crucial, whether scaling a mountain or climbing the craggy cliffs of the spiritual life. Our survival depends on how well we hang on—and what we hang on to.

There are some, however, who are slipping. They are losing their grip on what the Bible has to say about such spiritual disciplines as

- keeping our priorities straight
- staying involved with others
- striving for purity
- maintaining our integrity
- cherishing our families

This study will help equip you to hang on to the timeless truth of God's Word in a changing, drifting, and wind-whipped world. In our "anything goes" society, our hold on the Rock needs to be stronger than ever, which is why these studies are so important. They form fixed points that keep us from drifting aimlessly. God's eternal principles must be firmly grasped and communicated afresh if we hope to survive.

If you are looking for a few essentials to grab hold of as your world seems to be spinning by, almost out of control, these studies are just for you.

Chuck Swindoll

PUTTING TRUTH INTO ACTION

Knowledge apart from application falls short of God's desire for His children. He wants us to apply what we learn so that we will change and grow. This study guide was prepared with these goals in mind. As you go through the following pages, we hope your desire to discover biblical truth will grow as your understanding of God's Word increases and that you will be encouraged to apply what you've learned.

To assist you in your study, we've included a section called **Living Insights** at the end of each lesson. These exercises will challenge you to study further and to think of specific ways to put your discoveries into action.

There are many ways to use this guide—in personal devotions, group studies, discussions with friends and family, and Sunday school classes. And, of course, it's an ideal study aid when you're listening to its corresponding *Insight for Living* radio series.

To benefit most from this study guide, we would encourage you to consider it a spiritual journal. That's why we've included space in the **Living Insights** for recording your thoughts and discoveries. We hope you'll return to those sections often for review and encouragement as you continue to grow in your walk with Christ.

Ken Gire
Coauthor of Text

Gary Matlack
Coauthor of Text
Author of Living Insights

Essentials in an Aimless World

STRENGTHENING *Your* GRIP

Chapter 1

STRENGTHENING YOUR GRIP ON PRIORITIES

1 Thessalonians 2:1–13

Put first things first
and we get second things thrown in:
put second things first
and we lose *both* first and second things.
—C. S. Lewis[1]

Oh, the tyranny of "second things"! They scream for our attention, deafening us to the real priorities. And being Christians doesn't make us immune.

Take the way we minister, for example. Most churches have no problem getting a handle on priorities when they're just starting out. But later on—when success comes, when the congregation's needs outpace the ability to meet them all, when the church moves into its new facility, or when the winds of adversity kick up—the priority list can get blown away in a gust of confusion.

To make sure that list remains firmly in our grasp, we must strengthen our grip on four priorities—priorities that should characterize our churches as well as our personal lives.

Four Priorities That Characterize a Vital Ministry

With time, churches can lose their vitality. Instead of allowing God to stretch and shape them into living communities of believers, many congregations petrify in traditionalism. Maintaining programs becomes more important than ministering to people, and the result is an ingrown, stagnant clique.

1. C. S. Lewis, *The Quotable Lewis*, ed. Wayne Martindale and Jerry Root (Wheaton, Ill.: Tyndale House Publishers, 1989), p. 496.

In his letter to the Thessalonian believers, Paul shows us how to keep our ministries vibrant and alive in Christ.

1. Our Foundation Must Be Biblical

The foundation of Paul's message was the gospel.

> For you yourselves know, brethren, that our coming to you was not in vain, but after we had already suffered and been mistreated in Philippi, as you know, we had the boldness in our God to speak to you the gospel of God amid much opposition. For our exhortation does not come from error or impurity or by way of deceit; but just as we have been approved by God to be entrusted with the gospel, so we speak, not as pleasing men but God, who examines our hearts. (1 Thess. 2:1–4)

Had you sat among the worshipers in Thessalonica, you would have heard the clear and consistent declaration of God's Word, not a preacher's idle ramblings or opinions. The gospel of Christ was the foundation upon which the apostle built his exhortations and reproofs, making his teaching sure and dependable.

In contrast, whenever a church concentrates on pleasing people instead of God, its spiritual structure begins to wobble. God's Word is our only infallible blueprint. It provides rock-solid principles for every area of ministry: vision, educational curriculum, counseling, leadership, music, missions, and sermons. A ministry built on something other than the Word of God is headed for spiritual collapse.

If you skip down to verse 13, you'll see how the Thessalonians responded to Paul's preaching.

> And for this reason we also constantly thank God that when you received from us the word of God's message, you accepted it not as the word of men, but for what it really is, the word of God, which also performs its work in you who believe.

When God's Word is proclaimed, God's people are fed—and that includes the pastor. God's truth falls like a seed on fertile soil. Once received, it takes root in our lives, grows, and produces fruit. Everyone benefits. Everyone is nurtured.

How receptive is the soil of your heart to His Word? Are there any rocks or weeds that keep it from taking root? If so, won't you submit yourself to the Gardener's hoe and allow His Word to perform its work in your life? It could turn a dry walk with God into a dynamic one, a fruitless existence into a fruitful adventure.

2. *Our Application Must Be Authentic*

God's Word, however, isn't taught in a vacuum. It does its work among real people with real needs. That's why authenticity is essential in ministry. Paul understood this. Reflecting on those days he spent with the Thessalonian church, the apostle recalls that he

> never came with flattering speech, as you know, nor with a pretext for greed—God is witness—nor did we seek glory from men, either from you or from others, even though as apostles of Christ we might have asserted our authority. (vv. 5–6)

Neither egotism nor exploitation marred Paul's ministry to the Thessalonians. He didn't have one hand around their shoulders and the other in their pockets. He had no hidden agenda for plugging his latest book, touting his success as a church planter, or begging for money to keep his ministry alive. He was genuine, sincere, upfront, transparent.

Likewise, our ministries and lives must be free of deception and the drive to impress. We must be real, without hypocrisy and without hype. Authenticity means admitting we're not perfect. Paul wasn't afraid to divulge his struggles and weaknesses; he knew that his humanness was the very avenue through which Christ's work would be revealed (see 1 Thess. 2:2; 1 Cor. 2:1–5; 2 Cor. 12:7–10; 1 Tim. 1:15). None of us "has it all together"; we're all in process. So let's allow others to see beyond our Sunday best to the parts of our lives that still need work.

3. *Our Attitude Must Be Gracious*

Paul also put a priority on being gracious—full of tenderness and compassion.

> But we proved to be gentle among you, as a nursing mother tenderly cares for her own children. Having thus a fond affection for you, we were well-pleased to impart to you not only the gospel of God but also our own lives, because you had become very dear to us. (1 Thess. 2:7–8)

Paul didn't bark commands like a drill sergeant; he tenderly cared for the Thessalonians like a mother nursing her infant. Present-day evangelicalism could use a lot more gentleness and compassion. Pastors should be more than vending machines for the truth; they need to nurture and feed God's family.

Having begun with the tenderness of a mother, Paul now shifts to the loving guidance of a father.

> You are witnesses, and so is God, how devoutly and uprightly and blamelessly we behaved toward you believers; just as you know how we were exhorting and encouraging and imploring each one of you as a father would his own children. (vv. 10–11)

Just as we need a mother to nurse us, so we need a father to take us by the hand and show us the way. We need his strength not only to guide us but to pick us up when we stumble.

Don't get the idea from Paul's loving language that he was a spiritual softie; he was a warrior for the gospel. But he clearly distinguished between the spiritual enemy and people who were hurting and lost in darkness—imperfect believers needing grace. So he instructed the Thessalonians in the truth, but he also imparted his life to them.

4. Our Style Must Be Relevant

Paul invested himself deeply in the Thessalonians so they would "walk in a manner worthy of the God who calls you into His own kingdom and glory" (v. 12). Again, note the Thessalonians' response to his preaching.

> And for this reason we also constantly thank God that when you received from us the word of God's message, you accepted it not as the word of men, but for what it really is, the word of God, which also performs its work in you who believe. (v. 13)

The Thessalonians accepted the Word of God because of its relevance. It scratched where they itched. It healed where they hurt. It "performed its work"—made a difference—in their lives (v. 13b). Paul knew their culture well, and he presented the gospel with the day's issues in mind.

The Bible will never be obsolete; it will always be up-to-date. But our *culture* does change. Technology constantly gets upgraded.

Financial stability ebbs and flows. Fashions and tastes come and go at a whim.

So a ministry that wants to make an impact must be relevant. Without compromising the gospel, it must answer today's issues, not yesterday's. It must look forward more often than it looks back. And it must be willing to flex to stay up with the times, avoiding the restrictive bonds of traditionalism.

The Result of a Vital Ministry

A biblical foundation . . . authentic application . . . a gracious attitude . . . a relevant style. When we strengthen our grip on these priorities, Christianity becomes more than another item on our "to do" list. The reality of Christ soaks into our lives so deeply and completely that it changes the very chemistry of our being. And those around us cannot help but notice.

Living Insights STUDY ONE

Relevance is good. But when does relevance become compromise? We can conform to our culture so much that we distort God's Word in the process. In the interest of making biblical truth more palatable, more in line with the congregation's "felt needs," we can end up pleasing people instead of God. Perhaps you've seen this happen. Maybe you've even heard some of these comments:

- "People don't want to hear about sin these days; it's too negative. We need to uplift people—help them feel good about themselves."
- "With all the violence in today's world, the last thing we should be talking about is Jesus hanging on a bloody cross."
- "A virgin birth? Get real, this is the twentieth century."

Our challenge is to stay up with the times without looking down on the Word. Human sinfulness, God's love and forgiveness, and Jesus' miraculous birth apply just as much to the teenager who surfs the Internet as to the turn-of-the-century farmer.

Can you think of any examples from your experience in which relevance has crossed over the line into compromise? Think about your personal life as well as the life of your church. Is the Word of God still revered? Is purity being compromised for the sake of peer pressure? Is God still the focus? Or are people?

How can you stay involved in and empathetic toward your culture and still maintain an unwavering commitment to biblical truth? Consider such areas as:

- Movies
- Art
- Political involvement
- Your attitude toward non-Christians

Living Insights STUDY TWO

In this chapter we've studied four priorities that characterize a vital ministry. Let's make it more personal now. Have you given much thought to your individual priorities—the stars you steer by to keep from drifting aimlessly in a sea of "second things"?

Take some time to think about what's most important to you. Then write down five "non-negotiables" that you believe should characterize your life—no matter what.

-
-

-
-
-

Now, is your life structured to support these priorities? Have you made room in your schedule for them? How are you spending your money? What "second things" tend to pull you away?

What changes would you like to make?

Keep in mind that adjusting our priorities isn't always a matter of separating the good from the bad. Often, we just need to make room for the best.

Chapter 2

STRENGTHENING YOUR GRIP ON INVOLVEMENT

Acts 2:42–47; Romans 12:9–16; 1 Corinthians 12:20–27

Seventeenth-century poet and preacher John Donne once wrote:

> No man is an island, entire of itself; every man is a piece of the continent, a part of the main; if a clod be washed away by the sea, Europe is the less . . . ; any man's death diminishes me, because I am involved in mankind.[1]

Human beings were created for involvement, not isolation. God shaped us to fit together in relationship with Him and with each other. The Fall, though, bent that perfect union out of shape, leaving us either chafing against closeness to Him and others or straining to connect with Him and the people around us.

There is hope, however. Christ has come to soften our hearts, to help us yield to the relationships that can shape our lives into the pattern He designed. And where does He want this to happen? In His church. Remember what He said?

> "A new commandment I give to you, that you love one another, even as I have loved you, that you also love one another. By this all men will know that you are My disciples, if you have love for one another." (John 13:34–35)

Why, then, are so many Christians *un*involved? Too many of us show up for church without making meaningful connections—rarely getting beyond a shallow "Oh, I'm fine, thanks" and bolting for the parking lot during the closing prayer.

Whatever our reasons for detachment—self-sufficiency, shyness, insecurity, or busyness—God's Word encourages us and provides what we need to emerge from the shadows of isolation and linger in the light of involvement.

1. John Donne, as quoted in *Bartlett's Familiar Quotations*, 15th ed., rev. and enl., ed. Emily Morison Beck (Boston, Mass.: Little, Brown and Co., 1980), p. 254.

A Historical Perspective: Involvement in the Early Church

Throughout history, no church has better modeled involvement than the early church in Acts 2. It all started with Peter's sermon at Pentecost—three thousand Jews were saved. How's that for church growth? And they had no pastor, no bylaws, no sanctuary, and an incomplete Bible. Yet the members of this new congregation were more deeply involved with one another than almost any other group in history.

Even with the hindsight of two thousand years of church history, the latest technology, and shelves groaning under the weight of ministry books, few modern churches display the involvement of that first congregation.

> And they were continually devoting themselves to the apostles' teaching and to fellowship, to the breaking of bread and to prayer. (Acts 2:42)

The Greek term for *fellowship* is *koinōnia*, the root of which means "common." Drawn together by the thread of their common commitment to Christ, the early church became a tightly knit group. We might define fellowship, then, as genuine Christianity freely shared among God's family members.

Their Fellowship Analyzed

Acts 2:44–47 show us this *koinōnia*—this involvement—at work.

> And all those who had believed were together, and had all things in common; and they began selling their property and possessions, and were sharing them with all, as anyone might have need. And day by day continuing with one mind in the temple, and breaking bread from house to house, they were taking their meals together with gladness and sincerity of heart, praising God, and having favor with all the people. And the Lord was adding to their number day by day those who were being saved.

Notice that *everyone* participated in fellowship—the word *all* is used three times in verses 44–45. Not one person had an island mentality. They shared everything they had: property, possessions, food, even their lives. And they shared in a sincere, authentic way;

there was no coercion or contrivance. The more they shared, the closer they got.

Their Fellowship Expressed

The early church expressed its involvement in two ways. First, by sharing something *with others:* tangible things like money, food, and land. Second, by sharing with others *in something:* triumph, tragedy, joy, and grief.

Sometimes the best thing we can give is ourselves. Who can assign a dollar value to the tears we shed for someone else's loss? Or the time we give to listen to a friend vent his or her frustration? Or our applause upon learning of a peer's promotion?

Yet, even with the early church's example in Acts 2, some Christians may still feel that close fellowship is neither necessary nor beneficial for them personally. Perhaps that's why the apostle Paul also championed the cause of involvement.

A Present-Day Question: Why Get Involved?

Why get involved with others, anyway? Doesn't the Christian life really come down to us and God? In his letters to believers in Rome and Corinth, Paul provides two insightful answers: God commands it, and the body needs it.

God Commands It

Paul makes it clear that involvement with others is not an option; it's a mandate from God Himself.

> Let love be without hypocrisy. Abhor what is evil; cling to what is good. Be devoted to one another in brotherly love; give preference to one another in honor; not lagging behind in diligence, fervent in spirit, serving the Lord; rejoicing in hope, persevering in tribulation, devoted to prayer, contributing to the needs of the saints, practicing hospitality. Bless those who persecute you; bless and curse not. Rejoice with those who rejoice, and weep with those who weep. Be of the same mind toward one another; do not be haughty in mind, but associate with the lowly. Do not be wise in your own estimation. (Rom. 12:9–16)

How can we be devoted to others if we're not involved with them? How can we contribute to their needs if we remain at arm's length? How can we open our homes and our hearts if we never get to know each other? Clearly, God wants us to be involved. This takes more than just slapping backs on the way out of the worship service; it requires an investment in the lives of others. And it means accepting them with open arms, just as Christ accepted us (Rom. 15:7).

The Body Needs It

God commands involvement because He knows that's what it takes to build a healthy body of believers:

> But now there are many members, but one body. And the eye cannot say to the hand, "I have no need of you"; or again the head to the feet, "I have no need of you." (1 Cor. 12:20–21)

A hand is tough; an eye is tender. In order to be a healthy church, we need both. We need the eye to weep with the grieving, and the hand to support the stumbling.

> There should be no division in the body, but . . . the members should have the same care for one another. And if one member suffers, all the members suffer with it; if one member is honored, all the members rejoice with it. Now you are Christ's body, and individually members of it. (vv. 25–27)

We need each other for at least two specific reasons. First, *to dispel division* (v. 25a). Involvement breaks down cliques, mends fractures in fellowship, and fosters growth and care (see also Eph. 4:11–16).

Second, *to cultivate compassion* (1 Cor. 12:25b–26). Involvement allows us to both suffer and rejoice with others. This kind of caring is a sign of good health (see also Rom. 12:15; Heb. 13:3).

Three Essentials of Involvement

To encourage involvement in our churches, we need to maintain three essentials.

Spontaneity

Involvement should be voluntary and spontaneous, never

mandatory or contrived. For example, when you are drawn to a certain type of ministry, feel free to pursue it. Pick up the phone. Write a letter. Don't wait for permission or for a program to be developed. Use what God has given you to minister to the body.

That's a good word for those in church leadership too. You need to let people flow into a ministry that fits them, not hammer square pegs into round holes simply because you need help. Give people the freedom to get involved as God leads them.

Vulnerability

The word *vulnerable* means "capable of being . . . wounded, open to attack or damage."[2] We can't truly be involved with others if we don't open up and let them see our hurts and our weaknesses. Risky? Yes. But well worth the risk, when you discover the close fellowship that results when members of the body of Christ meet each other's needs.

Accountability

Involvement is also enriched by accountability. When we realize that our actions affect not only ourselves but the whole body, we don't mind being held accountable. We need relationships with people who will lovingly ask the tough, probing questions about our growth and purity.

So don't try to go it alone. Get involved. Sure, an uninhabited island might make a nice getaway. But would you really want to be stranded there for a lifetime?

Living Insights STUDY ONE

Are you involved?

"Involved? I couldn't be *more* involved," you might respond. "After all, just look at my schedule." OK, let's look at it.

7:30 A.M.	Help set up for Sunday morning service
8:30 A.M.	Finish preparing Sunday school lesson
9:30 A.M.	Sunday school
10:45 A.M.	Church
12:00 P.M.	Serve at new members' luncheon

2. *Merriam-Webster's Collegiate Dictionary*, 10th ed., see "vulnerable."

2:00 P.M.	Practice with ensemble for evening service
6:00 P.M.	Evening service
7:30 P.M.	Planning meeting for singles' retreat
9:00 P.M.	Write follow-up letters to visitors

And that's just Sunday! You've also got Monday night Bible study, visitation on Tuesday evenings, Wednesday prayer meeting, and a long list of social functions for the weekend. Your only free night is Thursday, and you need it to work on your Sunday school lesson.

Please, take a breath! And consider this: Involvement and busyness aren't necessarily synonyms. Sure, fellowship will often revolve around church programs, but just because our schedules are full doesn't mean we're involved in the lives of other believers. In fact, some people use busyness as an excuse to avoid getting close. They would rather stay moving than stop to share in the grief or celebration of another. Or to let someone comfort or encourage them.

There's nothing wrong with being busy—until it hinders real involvement. Sometimes we have to drop an activity or two to allow enough time to get to know someone.

Why not take a close look at your life right now? Are you really involved? What steps, if any, do you need to take to improve fellowship with those around you?

Living Insights STUDY TWO

It's true that no man is an island. But we still need to retreat into solitude from time to time to learn from the Lord one-on-one. What better way to improve our involvement with others than to grow in our love for Christ? Someone once said, "You can't minister out of a vacuum; you can't impart what you don't possess."

When's the last time you spent some sweet time with the Savior, all by yourself? If it's been awhile, do it now. Then go lavish His love on someone else who needs it.

Chapter 3

STRENGTHENING YOUR GRIP ON ENCOURAGEMENT

Hebrews 10:19–25

It's probably safe to say that Ruby Mae was the first person in the history of Cutter Gap, Tennessee, to rub citrus fruit on her face for cosmetic purposes.

Cutter Gap, after all, wasn't exactly known for its beauty secrets. One might go there to get expert advice on feuding or training coon dogs. But not for a makeover.

A visitor from Boston, however, had assured Ruby Mae that lemon juice would get rid of her freckles. It was worth a try. She couldn't do much about her strawberry red hair, but if she could get those freckles to fade, some of her self-doubt might disappear too.

So Ruby Mae took the long ride on horseback into town with Miss Alice. There were no lemons; she had to settle for oranges. As soon as she got home, she sliced one in half, rushed to the mirror, and started to rub . . . and rub . . . and rub. Her face, drooping with disappointment, looked out at her from the mirror.

"They won't come off, Miss Christy," she said to her friend and schoolteacher, who had been watching Ruby Mae frantically attempt a freckle-ectomy.

"You know, Ruby Mae," Christy said tenderly, "I never really noticed your freckles. I was always too busy looking at your beautiful eyes."

Ruby Mae looked at her reflection again, and a smile stretched across her sticky face.[1]

Sometimes, a little encouragement is worth more than all the oranges in the world. Some people, like Christy, seem to have a knack for it. They sense when another's spirit needs lifting. When the drought of depression or discouragement settles in, they refresh like a glass of iced tea in midsummer.

Encouragement, however, isn't limited to those with special abilities. God wants us all to encourage one another. And if Christians, who have access to the King of all encouragers, can't be uplifting, who can?

1. From a scene in the CBS television series *Christy*.

So, what do you say? Let's set aside our search for freckle faders and pick up some thoughts on encouraging others instead.

The Meaning of Encouragement

Our English word *encourage* comes from an Old French word that means "to put courage into." Webster says it means "to inspire with courage, spirit, or hope: hearten; to spur on: stimulate; to give help or patronage to: foster."[2]

As we take a look at encouragement, notice that it's a word of action—much more than a nice thought or simple flattery.

Our Source of Encouragement

For the Christian, encouragement is rooted in our relationship with Christ. Hebrews 10 reminds us of just a few of the things we have to be encouraged about.

> Since, therefore, brethren, we have confidence to enter the holy place by the blood of Jesus, by a new and living way which He inaugurated for us through the veil, that is, His flesh, and since we have a great priest over the house of God. . . . (vv. 19–21)

How wonderful. Can you really grasp that? *We have confidence to approach God.* It may help to remember the elaborate difficulty with which the people of the Old Testament had to come before God. From the time of Moses until Calvary, anyone wanting to approach God had to do so through a priest, formally and with much ceremony. Ever mindful of their sins, they had to slaughter a choice animal—a bloody and burdensome task—and offer it humbly before God as a sacrifice, the price of admission to His presence.

Now, though, because of Jesus' final sacrifice on the Cross, the door to the very throne room of God has been swung open. With Jesus as our great priest (v. 21), we no longer need to slaughter sheep and bulls on the altar. If we have trusted in His precious blood, we have access to God. No priest stands guard at the door to carry in our messages or to check our credentials, for it is Christ Himself who permits us entrance to the King.

2. *Merriam-Webster's Collegiate Dictionary*, 10th ed., see "encourage."

The Ministry of Encouragement

The writer of Hebrews tells us not only what we have but also what we should do:

> Let us draw near with a sincere heart in full assurance of faith, having our hearts sprinkled clean from an evil conscience and our bodies washed with pure water. Let us hold fast the confession of our hope without wavering, for He who promised is faithful; and let us consider how to stimulate one another to love and good deeds, not forsaking our own assembling together, as is the habit of some, but encouraging one another; and all the more, as you see the day drawing near. (vv. 22–25)

First, *let us draw near* (v. 22). We no longer need to tiptoe by the throne room of God or walk on eggshells in His presence. Instead, God has invited us to walk boldly to Him across the crimson carpet Jesus laid down for us.

Second, *let us hold fast* (v. 23). Hold fast to what? To "the confession of our hope"—the sure hope we have that God will keep His promises. It's as though the writer of Hebrews is saying, "We can rely on God completely. His Word doesn't change. So believe it; hold onto it."

Life was hard for these Hebrews. Their faith came at great cost: many were torn from their families, some were imprisoned, others were martyred. They needed something solid to cling to—the unwavering promises of God.

Third, *let us consider* (v. 24). Consider "how to stimulate one another to love and good deeds." Having encouraged us about all we possess in Christ, the writer now urges us to ponder how we can encourage others to live Christlike lives. We must avoid forsaking "our own assembling together" and, instead, work at "encouraging one another" (v. 25).

Notice that "forsaking the assembly" and "encouragement" are presented as opposites. God never meant Christians to isolate themselves. Rather, He has given all of us gifts and abilities so we can minister to one another. When we gather for worship and fellowship, we are creating an environment for encouragement.

The Greek word for *encourage* suggests close involvement with others. Coming from two words, *para* ("alongside") and *kalēo* ("to call"), encouragement means "to call alongside." Jesus used a form of the same word—*paraclete*—to describe the Holy Spirit, who guides us in our walk with God.

> "But the Helper, the Holy Spirit, whom the Father will send in My name, He will teach you all things, and bring to your remembrance all that I said to you." (John 14:26)
>
> "But I tell you the truth, it is to your advantage that I go away; for if I do not go away, the Helper shall not come to you; but if I go, I will send Him to you." (16:7)

An encourager, then, is a helper—someone who walks alongside us and keeps us on the road to Christ. Encouragers minister in a variety of ways. They listen. They affirm our contributions to the body. They put an arm around us. They smile. They challenge and stretch us. They even confront us when necessary.

When we encourage others, we share in the uplifting ministry of the Holy Spirit.

A Few Questions about Encouragement

To help us develop a pattern for encouraging others, let's ask three questions and let the Scriptures answer them.

1. Should we encourage others only on Sundays during the weekly "assembling together," or should it be more often?

   Answer: Day after day, as Hebrews 3:13 indicates.

   > Encourage one another day after day, as long as it is still called "Today," lest any one of you be hardened by the deceitfulness of sin.

2. Should we wait until we're asked to encourage, or should we watch for opportunities and take the initiative?

   Answer: Take the initiative, as Romans 14:19 implies.

   > So then let us *pursue* the things which make for peace and the building up of one another. (emphasis added)

3. Do we need to do something big to encourage someone, or is it possible to encourage with a word or two?

   Answer: Even a word, spoken sincerely, can lighten a load or lift the spirits, as Proverbs instructs us.

> There is one who speaks rashly like the thrusts of a
> sword,
> But the tongue of the wise brings healing. (12:18)
>
> Anxiety in the heart of a man weighs it down,
> But a good word makes it glad. (v. 25)
>
> A man has joy in an apt answer,
> And how delightful is a timely word! (15:23)

Sometimes, the people we feel can get by without encouragement may actually need it the most. Take David, for example. He was a warrior, poet, and future king of Israel. Yet he desperately needed encouragement when jealous King Saul tried to hunt him down like a wild beast.

> Now David became aware that Saul had come out to seek his life while David was in the wilderness of Ziph at Horesh. (1 Sam. 23:15)

News of Saul's plans must have pierced David's heart like a spear. But a friend was there to help patch up the wound.

> And Jonathan, Saul's son, arose and went to David at Horesh, and encouraged him in God. (v. 16)

Even David, a man after God's own heart, needed encouragement. And so do we.

Some Practical Suggestions for Encouraging Others

We can encourage those around us in a myriad of ways. Expressing appreciation for a friend's attention to details is one. Or how about thanking others for their faithfulness. Or acknowledging that employee's warm smile, positive spirit, and willingness to work late. We can even be an encourager by the way we live—how we model integrity, compassion, and diligence. The key is to look for ways to encourage.

And finally, as Paul tells us in Ephesians 4:29, remember that words have power—to wither someone's spirit or water it with God's grace.

> Let no unwholesome word proceed from your mouth, but only such a word as is good for edification according to the need of the moment, that it may give grace to those who hear.

If more of us would encourage, maybe others would be able to stop staring at their freckles and turn their lovely eyes to the Father.

Living Insights — STUDY ONE

> If Thy law had not been my delight,
> Then I would have perished in my affliction.
> I will never forget Thy precepts,
> For by them Thou hast revived me.
> (Ps. 119:92–93)

God's Word encourages. If you don't believe that, just ask the psalmist, to whom God's Word was like a cool breeze in the blazing desert of despair.

The Bible is brimming with encouraging truths about God. His love for us. His faithfulness. His forgiveness. His sovereignty. His grace in saving us and allowing us to participate in His ministry. His power to change us into Christ's image.

Take a moment to examine the following passages. What encouragement can you draw from each of them about living the Christian life?

Psalm 8 ______________________________

____

____

Matthew 28:18–20 ______________________________

____

____

Romans 8:31–39 ______________________________

____

____

2 Corinthians 4:7–18 ______________________________

____

____

Galatians 2:20 ______________________________

Ephesians 1:3–14 ______________________________

Don't keep all that refreshing truth to yourself! Share one or more of these passages with someone you know who needs a boost.

Living Insights STUDY TWO

Some people have a misconception about encouragement. They think that, to be an encourager, one has to be a glad-hander, a slap-you-on-the-back extrovert, always ready with a joke or story to lift others out of the doldrums. How inaccurate!

Some of the best encouragers are quiet, unassuming people. They simply show up to help. They smile and whisper, "I prayed for you this morning." Though they often say nothing, they speak volumes with a hug or an arm around the shoulder. And they silently instruct through their consistent walk with the Savior.

Take Barnabas, for example. The apostles nicknamed him "Son of Encouragement." Acts 4:36–37 suggests that he encouraged other believers, not with words, but by giving generously to the church.

Know anyone who needs encouragement this week? How can you provide it in a quiet but powerful way? Can you write a short letter? Photocopy and send an uplifting article? Simply sit with someone? List a few ideas of your own.

Chapter 4

STRENGTHENING YOUR GRIP ON PURITY

1 Thessalonians 4:1–5; Matthew 18:15–17

Sex is supreme." . . . "Follow your feelings." . . . "Do whatever gives you pleasure." . . . "Purity? That went out with the Puritans."

These are the slogans of a sex-obsessed society—our society. They pulse from the media like a strobe light, mesmerizing us into a state of moral apathy. Talk shows spotlight all the twisted paths people take to find sensual satisfaction. Sitcoms depict abstinence as fit only for the undesirable or immature. And advertisers blatantly seduce us into buying everything from cologne to cars.

But before we burn the media at the stake, we have some confessing of our own to do, don't we? Far too many Christians have bought into the "pursue pleasure at all costs" philosophy and model it with unsettling skill.

Take our marriages, for example. The difference between the national divorce rate and that for Christians is practically imperceptible. Or consider our leaders—some ministers create as much scandal as any movie star. Or how about our priorities? Many churches no longer place holy living at the top of the list.

Too many Christians, it seems, have followed the world's formula for living, thinking it's the only realistic choice in today's culture. But it's not. Purity, as Paul says in Romans 6, is a powerfully real alternative:

> Therefore do not let sin reign in your mortal body that you should obey its lusts, and do not go on presenting the members of your body to sin as instruments of unrighteousness; but present yourselves to God as those alive from the dead, and your members as instruments of righteousness to God. (vv. 12–13)

Some of us may be thinking that it was easier to follow Paul's charge for purity in the first century. The culture back then wasn't nearly as morally decayed as ours, right?

Has history got news for us.

Moral Erosion: A Historical Fact

True, there were no talk shows in Paul's day; no pornographic videos. No MTV or raunchy rap tunes. But the seductive whispers of immorality still reached the ears of both the Roman and Greek cultures, as commentator William Barclay reveals.

> In Rome for the first five hundred and twenty years of the Republic there had not been a single divorce; but now under the Empire, as it has been put, divorce was a matter of caprice. As Seneca said, "Women were married to be divorced and divorced to be married." In Rome the years were identified by the names of the consuls; but it was said that fashionable ladies identified the years by the names of their husbands. Juvenal quotes an instance of a woman who had eight husbands in five years. Morality was dead.
>
> In Greece immorality had always been quite blatant. Long ago Demosthenes had written: "We keep prostitutes for pleasure; we keep mistresses for the day-to-day needs of the body; we keep wives for the begetting of children and for the faithful guardianship of our homes." So long as a man supported his wife and family there was no shame whatsoever in extra-marital relationships.[1]

If Paul stepped into the 1990s, he might gawk at our technology, but he wouldn't be surprised at our depravity. Immorality, after all, was just as rampant in his day. That's why he wrote to the Christians in Thessalonica: to warn them about letting the poison of sexual immorality seep into the church.

Moral Purity: An Attainable Goal

After ministering for only a few weeks among the Thessalonians, Paul had been able to impart to them the life-changing truth of the gospel of Christ. But his purpose was not simply to chalk up as many converts as he could; he wanted to teach them

1. William Barclay, *The Letters to the Philippians, Colossians, and Thessalonians*, rev. ed., The Daily Study Bible Series (Philadelphia, Pa.: Westminster Press, 1975), p. 199.

to "walk in a manner worthy of the God who [had called them] into His own kingdom and glory" (1 Thess. 2:12).

Now he urges them to live out their high calling by making their purity shine in a darkened world.

> Finally then, brethren, we request and exhort you in the Lord Jesus, that, as you received from us instruction as to how you ought to walk and please God (just as you actually do walk), that you may excel still more. For you know what commandments we gave you by the authority of the Lord Jesus. For this is the will of God, your sanctification; that is, that you abstain from sexual immorality. (1 Thess. 4:1–3)

Paul's words amount to more than a general request for decent living. He wants the Thessalonians to *excel* in godliness. And he leaves no doubt that sexual purity "is the will of God" (v. 3). For by abstaining from sexual immorality, we demonstrate that we are "sanctified," which means set apart or distinct. The practice of purity causes us to stand out from the world like a diamond against black velvet.

The Greek word translated "sexual immorality" is *porneia*; from its root we get our word *pornography*. Thomas Constable's definition of this broad term is helpful in understanding Paul's exhortations.

> Christians are to avoid and abstain from any and every form of sexual practice that lies outside the circle of God's revealed will, namely adultery, premarital and extramarital intercourse, homosexuality, and other perversions. The word *porneia*, translated "sexual immorality," is a broad one and includes all these practices. The Thessalonians lived in a pagan environment in which sexual looseness was not only practiced openly but was also encouraged. In Greek religion, prostitution was considered a priestly prerogative, and extramarital sex was sometimes an act of worship. To a Christian the will of God is clear: holiness and sexual immorality are mutually exclusive. No appeal to Christian liberty can justify fornication.[2]

2. Thomas L. Constable, "1 Thessalonians," in *The Bible Knowledge Commentary*, New Testament edition, ed. John F. Walvoord and Roy B. Zuck (Wheaton, Ill.: Scripture Press Publications, Victor Books, 1983), p. 701.

Paul does more than tell us what *not* to do. He also issues a positive command.

> That each of you know how to possess his own vessel in sanctification and honor, not in lustful passion, like the Gentiles who do not know God. (vv. 4–5)

To "possess our vessels" means to control our bodies. We Christians sometimes so emphasize the spiritual side of our walk with God that we forget our bodies belong to Him too (see Rom. 6:12–13; 12:1; 1 Cor. 6:15–20; 9:27). So Paul reminds us that we're to be our body's master, not its slave. This means we don't *have* to give in to every urge that comes along. How different from the pagans of Paul's day and ours, who follow their lusts instead of the Lord.

With the Holy Spirit now working in us, we have the power to resist, the power to say "NO!" We can take an alternate route instead of the one that passes by the adult video store. We can grocery shop without stopping at the magazine stand to ogle the covers. We can say, "No, I'm married," or "No, I'm waiting until marriage," when we're tempted to compromise our purity for a flash of passion.

We are not meant to ignore our sexual feelings; rather, we need to become students of how physical stimuli affect our minds and bodies. Satan knows our desires. How much more, then, should we know them, and keep them ever before the Lord for His protection.

Next, Paul points out that purity comes down to making wise choices.

> Examine everything carefully; hold fast to that which is good; abstain from every form of evil. (1 Thess. 5:21)

We need to research that movie before rushing off to the theater—read some reviews, talk to others who have seen it. The same goes for television shows and music. We need to do more than just watch and listen. We need to ask whether we *should* watch and listen.

That's not legalism; that's wisdom. We're not suggesting a boycott of all movies and music. But each one of us should know our limits and weaknesses and avoid anything that trips us up in our walk with Christ, keeping our eyes fixed on Him (see also Titus 2:11–14; Heb. 12:1–2; 1 Pet. 1:13–16).

Purity is a conscious choice; it doesn't just happen. But what if Christians follow their passions into an impure lifestyle?

Moral Correction: A Biblical Mandate

Church discipline. The phrase conjures up all sorts of images and feelings—sullen-faced legalists, strict conformity to every jot and tittle, loveless judgment. How unfortunate, because these impressions come from an inaccurate, unbalanced understanding of Scripture.

God never intended church discipline to be used like a black boot of tyranny, stomping on anyone who can't keep up with the march. It's actually a last resort, meant to keep the body of Christ pure and to lovingly restore those living in immorality.

Well before the birth of the church at Pentecost, Jesus gave His disciples instructions on how to approach a sinning brother or sister in Christ and, if necessary, apply church discipline.

> "And if your brother sins, go and reprove him in private; if he listens to you, you have won your brother." (Matt. 18:15)

Step one: Go yourself. Jesus' words don't give us license to follow every member of the congregation around like a secret agent, waiting for someone to slip up. But if we see others living a lifestyle that's destructive to them and potentially harmful to the body of Christ, we should lovingly confront them in person and in private (see also Gal. 6:1; Eph. 4:15).

Confrontation can be uncomfortable. But if more of us would take this first step, instead of gossiping or letting our disapproval fester, we might see more Christians restored and more churches purified.

What if the offender rejects the confronter and persists in his or her lifestyle?

> "But if he does not listen to you, take one or two more with you, so that by the mouth of two or three witnesses every fact may be confirmed." (Matt. 18:16)

Step two: Take someone with you—not to gang up on the person but to confirm the accusations through the objectivity of others. Perhaps then, the individual will acknowledge his or her sin, repent of it, and thus help purify the body.

What if step two is unsuccessful? Jesus says,

> "And if he refuses to listen to them, tell it to the church." (v. 17a)

Step three: Make it a matter of public record to the church. This doesn't necessarily mean bringing the person in front of the whole congregation for discipline. Depending on the circumstances, the problem may best be handled with a group of elders or other officers who represent the congregation.

And finally,

> "if he refuses to listen even to the church, let him be to you as a Gentile and a tax-gatherer." (v. 17b)

Step four: Break off fellowship with this person until he or she comes around. That sounds harsh, doesn't it? Yet even the apostle Paul, a champion of grace and compassion, instructed the Corinthians to remove an unrepentant adulterer from their midst (1 Cor. 5:1–2, 5–7). This drastic measure apparently worked, bringing the offender to repentance and back into the fold (2 Cor. 2:6–8).

Dietrich Bonhoeffer revealed the heart of church discipline.

> Ultimately, we have no charge but to serve our brother, never to set ourselves above him, and we serve him even when we must speak the judging and dividing Word of God to him, even when, in obedience to God, we must break off fellowship with him. We must know that it is not our human love which makes us loyal to the other person, but God's love which breaks its way through to him only through judgment. Just because God's Word judges, it serves the person.[3]

Remember, though church discipline may be unpleasant, its ultimate purpose is to purify the body and bring sinning Christians to repentance and back into the community of faith.

Moral Inventory: A Look Inward

Before we're fooled into thinking that purification only applies to those involved in obvious, public sin, we need to remember that we all need purifying. That's why Jesus died for us. His blood makes us pure in God's sight, and His Spirit and Word give us what we need to walk in daily purity. Sure, we fail. But Jesus doesn't; He's

3. Dietrich Bonhoeffer, *Life Together*, trans. John W. Doberstein (San Francisco, Calif.: Harper and Row, Publishers, 1954), p. 107.

always there to forgive us, to clean us, to bring us back to Himself.

> If we confess our sins, He is faithful and righteous to forgive us our sins and to cleanse us from all unrighteousness. (1 John 1:9)

If we're going to change society's slogans, we first have to adopt a new slogan for ourselves: "Choose purity."

Living Insights STUDY ONE

On the road to spiritual maturity, all kinds of distractions tempt us to veer into impurity. What about you? Have you made purity a deliberate choice in your life? Or are your sensual desires in the driver's seat? Do you find yourself drifting toward the same old destructive thoughts and habits? List one that you're struggling with right now.

____

____

What lifestyle changes can you make to restore purity in that area? Here are a few suggestions. Place a check beside any you think might help, or write out your own strategy. Be sure to get specific and personal with the ones that apply to you. Otherwise, you may have trouble getting your plan off the paper and into action.

- Avoid exposing your eyes to certain things you shouldn't see. Examples: ______________________________________

  ____

- Study God's Word to know more about what it says regarding your particular struggle.
  Passages: ______________________________________

  ____

- Make yourself accountable to a loving and empathetic friend. Name: ______________________________________

- Say no one time; then again, and again, until it gets easier.

Say no to: ____

____

- Talk to your pastor or a counselor if the battle has gone on too long.
  Appointment scheduled for: ______________________________

  ____

- Other: ____

____

____

____

As basic as it sounds, don't forget prayer. Expressing our complete dependence on God is the first step to recovery (see John 15:4–5).

Living Insights STUDY TWO

We love quick fixes, don't we? Drive-through windows, fax machines, computers, microwaves, cellular phones, and cable television have conditioned us to think, "If I can't get it now, it's not worth having."

We often choose immorality because it seems to provide the most immediate and gratifying results. Actually, though, the more we give in, the more those patterns of impure living become ingrained in our lives. And the more destruction they inflict.

The Christian life wasn't designed to be a quick fix. The apostle Paul described it as a battle, a race, and a fight (see Eph. 6:10–20; 1 Cor. 9:24–27). The victory is assured, but the process is often draining.

If you're ready to unstrap the armor, hang up the cleats, or toss in the towel, stop and make a quick list of what God has accomplished in your Christian life.. You might be surprised to find that, over the long haul, things *are* getting better.

Maybe sin bothers you more than it used to; you're not as comfortable with it. Perhaps you're a kinder, gentler person than you once were. Do you have a desire to please God and serve others?

Has your love for God's Word increased? Jot down whatever comes to mind.

____

____

____

____

____

____

You see? There is progress, though sometimes imperceptible, in the struggle. Some of our greatest blessings and closest encounters with God come during seasons of spiritual struggle. Just ask Jacob, who wrestled all night with an angel on the banks of the Jabbok River (Gen. 32:22–32). "I have seen God face to face," he said, "yet my life has been preserved" (v. 30). And he limped away, the possessor of a new blessing and new name—Israel.

Maintaining purity isn't a spectator sport. It requires us to walk onto the mat and participate in the match. But if the wrestling pulls us closer to the face of our heavenly Father, the struggle is worth it.

Chapter 5

Strengthening Your Grip on Money

1 Timothy 6:3–19

I wouldn't mind strengthening my grip on money" we might say, ". . . a whole briefcase full!" Well, we can dream, can't we?

This chapter won't offer any get-rich-quick formulas. No lucky lottery numbers or stock tips here. What we will find, however, is help in getting a firm grasp on what the Bible says about money.

Now, don't worry. This isn't your basic "shame on you if you're not tithing" message. Scripture has much more to say about this topic than simply how to fill the offering plate. It provides principles for spending, sharing, saving, and investing. The Bible also tells us how to view money in relation to God and how to use it for His glory.

The apostle Paul knew that no one, not even himself as a Christian leader, was exempt from the temptation to misuse money. So in 1 Timothy 6, Paul reminds his young protégé, Timothy, that everyone, regardless of financial status, needs to develop the right attitude toward money. *Everyone*—which includes those who are not rich (vv. 6–8), those who want to get rich (vv. 9–10), and those who are rich (vv. 17–19).

A Reminder to Those Who Are Not Rich

From a biblical point of view, money itself is amoral—neither good nor bad. It's our *attitude* toward money and how we use it that determines the issue of morality or immorality. Scripture also shows that there is no inherent godliness in either wealth or poverty. The Bible abounds with godly people who were poor—for example, John the Baptizer (Matt. 3:4) and the widow who gave her last penny to the temple treasury (Mark 12:42); as well as godly individuals of great wealth—Abraham (Gen. 24:34–35) and Job (Job 1:1–3), for instance. Again, rich or poor doesn't matter to God; what He's concerned with is the heart (see Lev. 19:15; Prov. 22:2).

And it is the heart that Paul confronts in 1 Timothy 6. In Paul and Timothy's day, some unscrupulous people apparently saw religion as a way to make money (vv. 3–5). But the richest prize of all, says Paul, is a godly life, regardless of the size of our wallets.

> But godliness actually is a means of great gain, when accompanied by contentment (v. 6).

In other words,

Godliness + Contentment = Great Gain

You won't find this formula for success in *Forbes* or *Money* magazines. Yet this is the only kind of wealth that can't be consumed by rust or stolen by thieves (see Matt. 6:19–20). A consistent and authentic walk with God *plus* an attitude of satisfaction and inner peace . . . that's what constitutes true wealth.

Quite a different message from the one the world's sending, isn't it? Advertisers thrive on discontentment. Every television commercial or magazine ad we see screams, "Why settle for what you've got, when you can have more?" Our old deodorant was just fine, until we discovered one that promises to advance our careers. And that computer you purchased only a year ago? Practically obsolete. Just upgrade to this new system, just drive this car, just wear these jeans, just use this toothpaste . . . and you'll be happier, healthier, and more popular. And you'll meet only beautiful, shapely people.

Paul, however, says, "Be content. Stop striving for more; be satisfied and at peace with what you have." How do we do that?

The first half of the answer is found in 1 Timothy 6:7.

> For we have brought nothing into the world, so we cannot take anything out of it either.

First, *we need to look at life with an eternal perspective*. You can't take it with you, as they say. We wiggle our way into this world naked and empty-handed, and we leave the same way (see Job 1:21). Have you ever seen a hearse pulling a U-Haul or a corpse carrying luggage? When we die, we leave our possessions, whether little or much, behind. That's why Paul tells us in Colossians 3:2 to "set your mind on the things above, not on the things that are on earth."

When the eternal means more to us than the material, we just might realize we don't need as much as we thought we did.

> And if we have food and covering, with these we shall be content. (1 Tim. 6:8)[1]

1. The word *covering* in verse 8 is a general term for "anything that serves as a cover and hence as a protection. Chiefly *clothing* . . . but also *house*." Walter Bauer, *A Greek-English Lexicon of the New Testament and Other Early Christian Literature*, 2d ed. Revised and augmented by F. Wilbur Gingrich and Frederick W. Danker, from Walter Bauer's 5th ed., 1958 (Chicago, Ill.: University of Chicago Press, 1979), p. 753. See also Matthew 6:24–34.

So, second, *we need to enjoy the essentials with simple acceptance*. What are the essentials? Food and covering. With these we should be satisfied, as Paul himself learned.

> Not that I speak from want; for I have learned to be content in whatever circumstances I am. I know how to get along with humble means, and I also know how to live in prosperity; in any and every circumstance I have learned the secret of being filled and going hungry, both of having abundance and suffering need. I can do all things through Him who strengthens me. (Phil. 4:11–13)

Contentment may not come naturally, but it can be learned with Christ's help and in His strength.[2]

A Warning to Those Who Want to Get Rich

Now Paul shifts his attention from the non-rich to the want-to-be-rich—those in hot pursuit of the proverbial pot of gold at the end of the rainbow.

> But those who want to get rich fall into temptation and a snare and many foolish and harmful desires which plunge men into ruin and destruction. (1 Tim. 6:9)

That little word *want* in verse 9 seems tame enough, but it can be translated as a strong craving for something.[3] For these people, the pursuit of money is more than a passing fancy; it's a passionate obsession. Paul gives a series of stern warnings to all those whose eyes are filled with the glint of gold:

First: They fall into temptation and a snare.

Second: They fall into many foolish and harmful desires.

Third: Those things plunge them into ruin and destruction.

Not too encouraging, is it? The Greek word for *plunge* appears only here and in Luke 5:7, where it refers to a sinking boat. In the midst of a full-sailed pursuit of riches, a person's life can take on

2. Contextually, the "all things" of Philippians 4:13 probably refers to verse 12, which includes being able to live in the broad spectrum of circumstances ranging from poverty to prosperity.

3. A. Duane Litfin, "1 Timothy," in *The Bible Knowledge Commentary*, New Testament edition, ed. John F. Walvoord and Roy B. Zuck (Wheaton, Ill.: Scripture Press Publications, Victor Books, 1983), p. 746.

water and go under in no time at all (see also Prov. 28:22).

Remember, though, money itself isn't the problem. Our attachment to it is what sinks us.

> For the love of money is a root of all sorts of evil, and some by longing for it have wandered away from the faith, and pierced themselves with many a pang. (1 Tim. 6:10)

Study this verse carefully—it does not tell us, as some say, that money is *the* root of *all* evil. It says the *love* of money is *a* root of *all sorts* of evil.

Two perils await those who long for money: first, they wander away; second, they heap all kinds of problems on themselves. Commentator Duane Litfin explains:

> [Wandering away] may mean that they had fallen into heretical teaching (cf. 2 Tim. 2:17–18) or simply that their spiritual fruitfulness had been choked off (cf. Luke 8:14) by their concern for riches. In either case, they had suffered for it, causing themselves to be pierced . . . with many griefs (lit., "pains").[4]

How do we escape such misery? Paul says, "Flee!"

> But flee from these things, you man of God; and pursue righteousness, godliness, faith, love, perseverance and gentleness. Fight the good fight of faith; take hold of the eternal life to which you were called, and you made the good confession in the presence of many witnesses. I charge you in the presence of God, who gives life to all things, and of Christ Jesus, who testified the good confession before Pontius Pilate, that you keep the commandment without stain or reproach until the appearing of our Lord Jesus Christ, which He will bring about at the proper time—He who is the blessed and only Sovereign, the King of kings and Lord of lords; who alone possesses immortality and dwells in unapproachable light; whom no man has seen or can see.

4. Litfin, "1 Timothy," p. 746.

> To Him be honor and eternal dominion! Amen. (1 Tim. 6:11–16)

In the midst of providing for our families, enjoying our possessions, and planning for our retirements, let's keep our hearts reserved for God. Our immortal Savior, not our silver, deserves our undivided love and attention.

Instructions for Those Who Are Rich

So much for those who want wealth. What about those who have it? Paul now tells Timothy how to shepherd those who are rich.

> Instruct those who are rich in this present world not to be conceited or to fix their hope on the uncertainty of riches, but on God, who richly supplies us with all things to enjoy. (v. 17)

The apostle directs three straightforward commands to the rich—two negative and one positive.

First: *Don't be conceited.* Along with money comes the temptation to look down on those who have less. We need to remember that everything we have comes from God, and He can increase it or remove it at His discretion. Haughtiness shouldn't replace humility simply because we have money.

Second: *Don't trust in your wealth for security.* As Proverbs 23:4–5 warns,

> Do not weary yourself to gain wealth,
> Cease from your consideration of it.
> When you set your eyes on it, it is gone.
> For wealth certainly makes itself wings,
> Like an eagle that flies toward the heavens.

Our only real security is in Jesus Christ, who never fails us.

Third: *Become a generous person.* Paul tells Timothy,

> Instruct them to do good, to be rich in good works, to be generous and ready to share, storing up for themselves the treasure of a good foundation for the future, so that they may take hold of that which is life indeed. (1 Tim. 6:18–19)

What a concept! God blesses some of us with riches, not so we can hoard it all, but so we can share it with others who are in need (see also Eph. 4:28). By giving generously, we walk with God in the path of life (see Ps. 16:11) and store up riches for ourselves in heaven.

Greed, on the other hand, takes us along a dark road and fills our hands with illusory treasures, warns our Lord in Luke 12:15.

> Beware, and be on your guard against every form of greed; for not even when one has an abundance does his life consist of his possessions.

An abundance of things doesn't equal an abundant life. Only one Person can supply that, as Jesus said of Himself.

> "I came that they might have life, and might have it abundantly." (John 10:10b)

Living Insights STUDY ONE

It comes on like a fever every time I walk into a computer store.

I usually feel it in the gut first—a fluttering sensation, like a case of the butterflies before an important speech. Then it works its way up the spine, causing my flesh to sprout goose bumps. My mouth gets dry. My eyes widen uncontrollably. And the next thing I know, I'm in a trance, wandering up and down the aisles like a kid turned loose in Toys R Us.

The dazzle of technology awakens my inner voice of discontentment, which now tries to persuade me that I can't live without these glittering goodies.

Oh, a laptop, says the voice. *No writer can be successful without a laptop. True, you hardly ever leave your office, but what if you suddenly started to travel? You would be . . . unequipped. Perish the thought! Not in today's age. You can't afford to be unequipped.*

Why, this one's twice as powerful as that outdated hunk of plastic sitting on your desk. Go ahead, touch it. That's right. Pick it up. See how light, how compact? And it has a color monitor. Glory, glory, welcome to the twenty-first century!

"Can I help you?" It usually takes a salesperson to snap me back to reality.

"No, uh, thanks. Just looking."

All right, so you can't afford a laptop. At least get some current software . . .

My home computer, actually, is not that outdated. It does everything I need it to do and beyond. So I possess more technology than I will ever use. I should be satisfied. But when I see all those new products displayed like shimmering stones in a jewelry store, my contentment goes right out the window.

Are you like I am in a computer store—always wanting the newest, the best, the most prestigious? Or are you satisfied with what you have? Think about it. And write down whatever thoughts, confessions, and resolutions come to mind. Grab a pen and paper, or your laptop computer, and get started. This could take some time. You might be amazed at how many wonderful things you already have to be thankful for.

Living Insights

STUDY TWO

"Flee materialism, and pursue godliness," Paul tells Timothy (see 1 Tim. 6:11). We're to run away from one thing, and run toward another. It's interesting that Paul didn't stop after just the first part. Apparently, simply avoiding falling in love with money is an insufficient plan of action.

Jesus, too, prescribed this two-pronged approach when He said, "Do not lay up for yourselves treasures upon earth . . . but lay up for yourselves treasures in heaven" and "seek first His kingdom and His righteousness" (Matt. 6:19–20; 33).

Pursue, lay up, seek. Action verbs, every one. Do you get the feeling that the secret to avoiding the materialism trap is to actively seek God? He knows that in our own strength, we can't possibly resist temptation. It's not enough to tighten our fists, clench our teeth, and mumble, "I will not love money, I will not love money." Rather, we need to transfer our love from money to God. If He is the object of our affection and joy, money can't be. As Jesus also said, "You cannot serve God and mammon" (Matt. 6:24).

Most of us would agree that getting rich takes commitment, hard work, planning, and perseverance. Yet how often we think that spiritual growth just "happens." It doesn't. It requires time with God, deliberate and consistent Bible study, and daily dependence on Him.

Are you seeking Him? Are you working as hard to know Him as you are to make ends meet? If not, start now. He's waiting. And, unlike other investments, He never loses interest.

Chapter 6

STRENGTHENING YOUR GRIP ON INTEGRITY

Psalms 75:5–7; 78:70–72

Some things have to be tested to be proven.

Dr. Evan O'Neill Kane knew that. The chief surgeon of New York City's Kane Summit Hospital had a theory that would revolutionize medicine. But it hadn't been tested.

In his thirty-seven years of operating, Dr. Kane had seen a number of deaths and disabilities resulting from general anesthesia: damage to patients with heart problems, acute allergic reactions, and so on. He believed its hazards outweighed the risks of actual surgery. In his studied opinion, most major operations could be done under local anesthesia—a safer, more reliable method, though an unproven one.

His experiment required a patient who could part with his or her appendix. For Dr. Kane, who had performed nearly four thousand appendectomies, the operation would be routine, except for one thing—the patient would be awake during the entire procedure.

Volunteers, understandably, were scarce. But that didn't discourage the surgeon. He found just the right person; and on February 15, 1921, Dr. Kane performed a flawless operation. With his usual deftness, he administered the anesthetic, removed the appendix, and sewed up the patient, who experienced only minor discomfort during surgery.

The patient, a sixty-year-old man, recovered remarkably well and progressed much faster than typical postoperative patients. He was released from the hospital after just two days.

Dr. Kane's theory about local anesthetic had passed the test. He must have been overjoyed about what this meant for the future of medicine. And he must have been relieved. For the patient was someone he knew very well. You see, Dr. Kane operated on himself.[1]

Some things have to be tested to be proven. Medical theories,

1. Adapted from Paul Aurandt, *More of Paul Harvey's The Rest of the Story*, ed. and comp. by Lynne Harvey (Toronto: Bantam Books, 1980), pp. 79–80.

athletic ability, even character traits—such as integrity. Since most of us, however, aren't willing to "operate" on ourselves to discover what we're made of, God allows life to administer the tests. And in the process, our integrity, or lack of it, comes to light.

How well do you think your integrity will hold up under testing? Let's find out.

Two Tests

Two conditions test the strength of our integrity—adversity and prosperity.

The Test of Adversity

Few things reveal how strong or weak we are like the strenuous course of adversity. As Solomon observed,

> If you are slack in the day of distress,
> Your strength is limited. (Prov. 24:10)

Just as a footrace tests the heart of a runner, adversity tests the strength of our character. The Christian life, though, isn't a fifty-yard dash. It's a marathon, with challenging hills, monotonous straightaways, and crowded turns.

How well do you run when life's uphill climbs get longer and steeper? When it's too tough to keep going, when you're tempted to drop out of the race, what do you do? How we respond exposes the condition of our character.

Who can forget the horror of the Oklahoma City explosion? A terrorist's bomb sheared off the front half of the Murrah Federal Building, snuffing out the lives of 170 people, including several children. Yet, in the midst of the carnage, character rose to the surface.

Rescuers worked around the clock, clawing through rubble for possible survivors. Families pulled together to comfort one another. Churches and relief organizations from around the country sent care packages. And federal agents launched a relentless investigation to bring the terrorists to justice. The character of people was the one thing the blast wasn't able to destroy.

Author and therapist Thomas Szasz makes a profound statement about the role of adversity in our lives.

> [This is the] simplest and most ancient of human truths: namely, that life is an arduous and tragic struggle; that what we call "sanity" . . . has a great

> deal to do with competence, earned by struggling for excellence; with compassion, hard won by confronting conflict; and with modesty and patience, acquired through silence and suffering.[2]

The name Job is synonymous beyond any other with suffering and adversity. Reading through the man's tearstained journal, we find ten fresh graves not far from his home. They are the graves of his children. Satan has taken them all away, along with everything else Job had—his livestock, his servants (Job 1:13–17), and finally, his health (2:7–8).

How did this blameless, upright, and God-fearing man (see 1:1; 2:3a) respond? He held fast to his integrity (2:3b, 9–10; 27:5; 31:6). But, as one of his not-so-comforting friends pointed out, a few flaws came to the surface as well.

> Then Eliphaz the Temanite answered,
> "If one ventures a word with you, will you become
> impatient?
> But who can refrain from speaking?
> Behold you have admonished many,
> And you have strengthened weak hands.
> Your words have helped the tottering to stand,
> And you have strengthened feeble knees.
> But now it has come to you, and you are
> impatient;
> It touches you, and you are dismayed." (4:1–5)

Does that mean Job failed the integrity test? No. Holding on to our integrity doesn't mean having to withstand adversity's flames with a smile on our face and a picture-perfect attitude. God knows our flesh is frail (see Ps. 103:14). What He looks for is the quality of our faith—that's what can emerge like refined gold. And if we're willing to submit to God's sovereign wisdom, He is just as deeply pleased with us as He was with Job (see Job 42:1–9).

The Test of Prosperity

Someone has said, "Money can't buy happiness, but it can make misery a lot more bearable." How often we sigh and think, "If I

2. Thomas Szasz, as quoted by Eugene H. Peterson in *A Long Obedience in the Same Direction* (Downers Grove, Ill.: InterVarsity Press, 1980), pp. 16–17.

only had more money." Believe it or not, though, prosperity tests our integrity just as harshly as adversity, sometimes more so.

Scottish essayist Thomas Carlyle once wrote: "Adversity is sometimes hard upon a man; but for one man who can stand prosperity, there are a hundred that will stand adversity."[3] In the midst of suffering, you see, there is one primary goal—survival. We're more dependent on God during trials; we're seeking His direction. But prosperity issues the challenge, "Can you still live for God when you have everything you want?" Adversity reduces life to the basics; prosperity complicates it by giving us plenty of things to depend on besides God.

Has this been a prosperous year for you? Perhaps years of hard work are finally paying off, and you can enjoy the sweet fruit of your labor. Be warned, though. Satan would love to spoil it all by letting you get puffed up with pride. As God told the boastful and wicked,

> "'Do not lift up your horn on high,
> Do not speak with insolent pride.'" (Ps. 75:5)

If you're prospering, God warns: *Don't be conceited.* Don't strut your stuff like a bull proudly tossing its horns.

One man who knew a lot about prosperity was Solomon. He had firsthand experience in letting it get between him and God, so his words are worth listening to.

> Let another praise you, and not your own mouth;
> A stranger, and not your own lips. . . .
> The crucible is for silver and the furnace for gold,
> And a man is tested by the praise accorded him.
> (Prov. 27:2, 21)

Surprisingly, our character is tested and proven, not so much by criticism, but by the praise and acclaim of others. And note, *others*—we're not to toot our own horns or coax compliments out of people. Rather than prize our success, we should applaud God's grace and accept it with humility and gratitude.

The Psalms give us another warning about prosperity: *Keep the right perspective.*

3. Thomas Carlyle, as quoted in *Bartlett's Familiar Quotations*, 15th ed., rev. and enl., ed. Emily Morison Beck (Boston, Mass.: Little, Brown and Co., 1980), p. 474.

For not from the east, nor from the west,
Nor from the desert comes exaltation;
But God is the Judge;
He puts down one, and exalts another.
(Ps. 75:6–7)

Whether in the valley or on the mountaintop, the tilt of the neck should be the same—we have to look up to see God. He is the judge over all the earth. He is the One, ultimately, who gives or takes away, who raises up or brings down (see 1 Sam. 2:7; Dan. 2:21).

A beautiful example of this is found in Psalm 78, which tells of God's taking David as a humble young shepherd and exalting him to the highest office in the land.

He also chose David His servant,
And took him from the sheepfolds;
From the care of the ewes with suckling lambs
He brought him,
To shepherd Jacob His people,
And Israel His inheritance.
So he shepherded them according to the integrity
of his heart,
And guided them with his skillful hands.
(vv. 70–72)

David wasn't a mover and a shaker. He wasn't climbing up the corporate ladder. Nor was he a child prodigy who stayed up nights dreaming of the presidency. He was just a blue-collar shepherd—but a shepherd with integrity. That's what separated him from the hirelings and the hucksters.

David's reputation for integrity of heart came not because he was always righteous or spiritually healthy, but because he continually put himself before the probing eye of God.

Search me, O God, and know my heart;
Try me and know my anxious thoughts;
And see if there be any hurtful way in me,
And lead me in the everlasting way.
(Ps. 139:23–24)

If we want to have the integrity David had, we, too, must continually bare our hearts before God. We must endure His scrutiny—and, if necessary, His correction.

For our integrity to be proven, we must submit ourselves to the scalpel of adversity or the probing light of prosperity, depending on our circumstances. That's when we'll find out what we're really made of.

Living Insights STUDY ONE

Has your integrity been put to the test lately? Have you been tempted to compromise in order to relieve the pain of adversity or retain the comfort of your possessions? Give some thought to your most recent trial. How did you do? What did you learn that will help you when the next test comes?

Living Insights STUDY TWO

Whom do you know who consistently models integrity? It may be someone you know very well—your spouse, a close friend, a superior or subordinate at work. Or it might be someone you've observed from a distance—a neighbor, your pastor, your child's teacher.

Write down some specific ways this person's integrity comes to the surface. Does he keep his promises? Does she stick to her values and convictions during the hard times? Does he seem unaffected by prosperity? Is she a genuine person, not talking one way and living another?

____

____

____

____

____

____

Why not take some time to write this person a note of thanks for living out integrity when so many others are merely talking about it? You never know. Your note might be what God uses to remind him or her that upright living really does make a difference.

Chapter 7

STRENGTHENING YOUR GRIP ON DISCIPLESHIP

Matthew 28:16–20; Mark 3:13–14; Luke 14:25–33

Time for a pop quiz. A disciple is:

a. Someone who has completed a ten-week Bible study course

b. A Christian leader

c. A knowledgeable Christian

d. A zealous Christian

e. A Christian who uses compact discs

Answer? None of the above. Surprised? Don't be. Never has a word been so overused yet so misunderstood. Then what is a disciple? The Greek word for *disciple* is *mathētēs*, which comes from the verb *manthanō*, meaning "to learn."

> A *mathētēs* was one who attached himself to another to gain some practical or theoretical knowledge, whether by instruction or by experience. The word came to be used both of apprentices who were learning a trade and of adherents of various philosophical schools.[1]

Eugene Peterson explains this word as it relates to our walk with Christ.

> *Disciple* (*mathētēs*) says we are people who spend our lives apprenticed to our master, Jesus Christ. We are in a growing-learning relationship, always. A disciple is a learner, but not in the academic setting of a schoolroom, rather at the work site of a craftsman.

1. Lawrence O. Richards, *Expository Dictionary of Bible Words* (Grand Rapids, Mich.: Zondervan Publishing House, Regency Reference Library, 1985), p. 226.

> We do not acquire information about God but skills in faith.[2]

Though scriptural knowledge is crucial to our faith, we need to remember that discipleship is relational. Disciples not only learn *about* their Master, they grow closer *to* Him. The historical Jesus—the baby who squirmed in a stable's straw, the boy who baffled teachers of the Law with His knowledge, the Healer who made lifeless limbs leap, the Savior who died on a rugged cross and walked out of His tomb—is also the "here-and-now" Jesus. He is *our* Healer, *our* Savior, *our* resurrected Lord.

The Cornerstone of Discipleship

Discipleship is more than just another program in the church. It is *the* program of Christ's church, as Matthew clearly shows us in his account of Jesus' final words on earth.

> The eleven disciples proceeded to Galilee, to the mountain which Jesus had designated. And when they saw Him, they worshiped Him; but some were doubtful. And Jesus came up and spoke to them, saying, "All authority has been given to Me in heaven and on earth. Go therefore and make disciples of all the nations, baptizing them in the name of the Father and the Son and the Holy Spirit, teaching them to observe all that I commanded you; and lo, I am with you always, even to the end of the age." (28:16–20)

"I'm leaving, but I'm going to continue my mission through you," Jesus told His followers. His mission? To "make disciples." In the Greek version of this passage, that's the only imperative verb. "Go," "baptizing," and "teaching" are all participles dependent on the main command to make disciples.

So if we're not making disciples—committed followers of Christ—we're neglecting our primary mission. But how can we know whether we're truly discipling people or just promoting programs? Let's return to the gospels for the answer.

2. Eugene H. Peterson, *A Long Obedience in the Same Direction* (Downers Grove, Ill.: InterVarsity Press, 1980), p. 13.

The Choosing of the Disciples

Matthew 28 illustrates a key principle of discipleship—multiplication. In Jesus' own ministry, He spent some of His time addressing crowds, but He focused most of His efforts on twelve men. They, in turn, were to pass His teaching on to others—no insignificant task. So choosing these men could not be left to a random recruiting project. Jesus needed to select each one personally.

> And He went up to the mountain and summoned those whom He Himself wanted, and they came to Him. . . . And He appointed the twelve: Simon (to whom He gave the name Peter), and James the son of Zebedee, and John the brother of James (to them He gave the name Boanerges, which means, "Sons of Thunder"); and Andrew, and Philip, and Bartholomew, and Matthew, and Thomas, and James the son of Alphaeus, and Thaddaeus, and Simon the Zealot; and Judas Iscariot, who also betrayed Him. (Mark 3:13, 16–19)

Did Jesus collect résumés and interview applicants, looking for the ideal candidates—educated, confident, successful? Hardly. As author Robert Coleman tells us, what stands out about Jesus' men isn't who they were, but who they were not.

> What is more revealing about these men is that at first they do not impress us as being key men. None of them occupied prominent places in the Synagogue, nor did any of them belong to the Levitical priesthood. For the most part they were common laboring men, probably having no professional training beyond the rudiments of knowledge necessary for their vocation. Perhaps a few of them came from families of some considerable means, such as the sons of Zebedee, but none of them could have been considered wealthy. They had no academic degrees in the arts and philosophies of their day. Like their Master, their formal education likely consisted only of the Synagogue schools. Most of them were raised in the poor section of the country around Galilee. Apparently the only one of the twelve who came from the more refined region of Judea was Judas

> Iscariot. By any standard of sophisticated culture then and now they would surely be considered as a rather ragged aggregation of souls.[3]

Encouraging, isn't it, that Jesus chose people just like us to be His original disciples. And notice why He chose them.

> And He appointed twelve, that they might be with Him, and that He might send them out to preach, and to have authority to cast out the demons. (vv. 14–15)

The progression here is important. First, Jesus selected His disciples. Why? So "they might be with Him." Doing the work of the ministry comes later—it is mentioned last in these verses. This shows that selection and association preceded proclamation and service. The disciples were involved *with* Jesus before they went into action *for* Jesus.

Today, we often get the cart before the horse. We need people to fill slots in church programs, so we toss them into the ministry mix before they're ready. Many barely know who Jesus is; some have spent little or no time with Him. So they wind up desperately trying to quench the spiritual thirst of others from an empty well.

Jesus simply invited His men to share life with Him. That's where discipleship, and all of ministry, begins. He offered no high-powered seminars, no well-equipped classrooms, no formal training on technique.

In case you're wondering if being with Jesus really can change a person, consider Peter and John's ministry a few years later.

After miraculously healing a lame man at the temple in Jerusalem, Peter and John boldly proclaimed Christ's salvation message (Acts 3:1–4), and five thousand men joined the church. However, the very mention of Christ incensed the Jewish leaders, so they dragged Peter and John to the court of Annas the high priest and demanded that they explain their behavior. Filled with the Holy Spirit, Peter turned the tables on the religious leaders and called them to account for their wrongful conviction and crucifixion of Christ (Acts 4:5–12).

How did the religious leaders respond?

3. Robert E. Coleman, *The Master Plan of Evangelism*, 2d ed. (Old Tappan, N.J.: Fleming H. Revell Co., 1964), pp. 22–23.

> Now as they observed the confidence of Peter and John, and understood that they were uneducated and untrained men, they were marveling, and began to recognize them as having been with Jesus. (v. 13)

The disciples—unsophisticated and coarse in the eyes of the religious leaders—could speak with boldness and conviction because they had been in the presence of the Lord. And even the unbelievers recognized it.

The Cost of Discipleship

How much does being Christ's disciple cost? Jesus lays out the expense in Luke 14.

> Now great multitudes were going along with Him; and He turned and said to them, "If anyone comes to Me, and does not hate his own father and mother and wife and children and brothers and sisters, yes, and even his own life, he cannot be My disciple." (vv. 25–26)

Hate our families? Can this be the same Jesus who told us to love our enemies? The same God who commanded us to honor our mothers and fathers? Yes. But we can't take His statement too far. Jesus isn't proposing literal hate here. Rather, He's stressing the priority of a relationship with Him. We must love Him more than anyone else, more than our own lives. A true disciple puts his or her walk with God above all other relationships.

That doesn't mean we lock ourselves in the closet with a Bible and never come out. Or that we withhold hugs from our kids or avoid romantic evenings with our spouses. Putting Jesus first means that, above all else, we seek to please Him. We make decisions according to His will, even if it causes tension, misunderstanding, or ridicule in our earthly relationships.

Don't hit that "total" button yet—there's more.

> "Whoever does not carry his own cross and come after Me cannot be My disciple. For which one of you, when he wants to build a tower, does not first sit down and calculate the cost, to see if he has enough to complete it? Otherwise, when he has laid a foundation, and is not able to finish, all who observe it

> begin to ridicule him, saying, 'This man began to build and was not able to finish.' Or what king, when he sets out to meet another king in battle, will not first sit down and take counsel whether he is strong enough with ten thousand men to encounter the one coming against him with twenty thousand? Or else, while the other is still far away, he sends a delegation and asks terms of peace. So therefore, no one of you can be My disciple who does not give up all his own possessions." (vv. 27–33)

Discipleship not only demands that we prioritize our relationships, it requires us to surrender our very lives to Christ's leadership. In Jesus' day, when a sentenced man "took up his cross," he was on his way to execution. The cross symbolizes death. In Jesus' case, it also illustrates sacrifice and surrender. Disciples "die" to their own lives, surrendering their goals and dreams to those of the Lord. And they're willing to loosen their grip on all they possess and allow God to use it to His glory.

Not exactly a warm-fuzzy idea, is it? And Jesus knows it. In His own ministry, He never begged people to follow Him. In fact, He did just the opposite. Fully aware that many hung around Him merely to satisfy their curiosity, gain His approval, or align themselves with Him for political gain, Jesus gave them the straight scoop on discipleship—it will cost you everything.

Expensive, you say? Yes, but your investment will yield eternal dividends.

Living Insights — STUDY ONE

Discussions about discipleship often revolve around form instead of function. Memorize a verse a day. Study a chapter a week. Meet one-on-one. Complete this course. Check off that activity.

Diligent study, fellowship, and church attendance all contribute to growing in Christ. But sometimes we see these activities as an end in themselves. Remember, the goal of discipleship is to know Christ better and to be like Him.

Do you feel that you know Jesus Christ better now than you did when you started your spiritual journey? Or has your walk with Christ dwindled to a dawdle?

If you're feeling at a standstill, don't frantically compile a list of "ten things to add to my already full schedule to make me a better Christian." Instead, focus on getting to know the Savior better. Plunge into some passages that will remind you of who He is, how available and faithful He is, and how much He loves you. Then let your commitments grow out of your time with Him. Feel free to record your thoughts as you work through the following suggested passages or others you come up with on your own.

Lamentations 3:22–23

Matthew 7:7–11

John 15:7–9

Other passages that speak to your heart:

Living Insights STUDY TWO

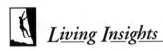

Perhaps your spiritual journey has been anything but stagnant. If so, then now is a good time to say with the psalmist, "I shall remember the deeds of the Lord; Surely I will remember Thy wonders of old" (Ps. 77:11).

Think about the day you began your walk with God. Now think about where you are today. Imagine the time in between as a journey across diverse terrain. You started out strolling through a meadow blanketed with green grass and clover. Mountain streams, it seemed, were everywhere, gurgling over glassy rocks and providing endless handfuls of icy refreshment.

Then came the desert, an oven of adversity. You prayed for water, but there was none. Then, parched, burned, and discouraged, you stumbled upon a spring ringed with palm trees and fed by a whispering waterfall. That oasis gave you the strength to go on.

You've had to climb a few craggy peaks, but the view at the top was always worth it. You've crossed mountains and valleys, rivers and rocks. Experienced rain and drought. Walked in darkness and light.

No, the journey of discipleship hasn't been one of the easiest journeys of your life. But look how far you've come. Take some time to retrace your steps. What has your adventure taught you about the following topics?

Victory

Defeat

Perseverance

God's Faithfulness

Character

Obedience ____

____

What two or three passages of Scripture have meant the most to you during your journey?

____

____

____

____

____

Who, besides God, has helped you along the way?

____

____

____

One day, you'll reach your heavenly home. For now, though, you're nourished, encouraged, and led by the most reliable Guide in the universe. He has never left your side. And He never will.

> Surely goodness and lovingkindness will follow
> me all the days of my life,
> And I will dwell in the house of the Lord
> forever. . . .
> So we Thy people and the sheep of Thy pasture
> Will give thanks to Thee forever;
> To all generations we will tell of Thy praise.
> (Ps. 23:6; 79:13)

Chapter 8

STRENGTHENING YOUR GRIP ON AGING

Psalm 90; Joshua 14:6–14

Are you getting old? In case you're not sure, you might want to examine the following list of symptoms. You can tell you're getting old when . . .

- the flight attendant offers you coffee, tea, or Milk of Magnesia;
- your back goes out more than you do;
- you sit in a rocking chair and can't get it started;
- everything hurts, and what doesn't hurt doesn't work;
- you sink your teeth into a juicy steak, and they stay there.

There's another way to tell—the value society places on you. Unfortunately, our mover-and-shaker culture doesn't highly esteem its senior citizens. In biblical times, however, the elderly were respected rather than ridiculed; gray hair was a shining crown of glory, not a label of uselessness (see Prov. 16:31).

Older people are like shimmering veins of silver running through society, just waiting to be mined. But when we abandon or neglect them, we leave untold riches buried in the dirt. And we are the poorer for it. So if you tend to look down your nose at the elderly, or if you feel you're too old to be useful, we hope this study will help you realize that age isn't a synonym for obsolescence. In fact, your most productive and significant years may be ahead of you.

Various Attitudes toward Aging

Before we look at the Bible's positive perspective on aging, let's understand several negative attitudes held by those who struggle with getting old.

Uselessness

"I'm over the hill" . . . "I'll just be in the way" . . . "I really don't have much to contribute anymore." Too many men and women believe that, like the old clunker in the garage, they belong to another era, that they don't quite fit in today's world. They look at their life as a rusty relic rather than a treasure trove of insight gathered from a wide array of experience.

Guilt

"I've blown it" . . . "If only I could do it all over again" . . . "If only I had a second chance." Some older folks look back over their lives feeling a burden of guilt. They constantly put themselves through self-designed penance for things they shouldn't have done or things they left undone. The pictures hanging on memory's walls line a haunted house instead of an inviting gallery.

Self-pity

Falling somewhere between blame and bitterness, self-pity cries out, "Nobody cares about me anymore" . . . "Nobody cares if I hurt" . . . "Nobody cares if I die." Self-pity banishes a person to solitary confinement rather than spurring one toward new freedom and involvement.

Fear

Many older people are afraid. Some fear trying to survive in a world that's moving too fast. Others fear the specter of fading health. Or being alone. Or becoming dependent. "What if . . ." and "I can't . . ." start a lot of their sentences. And the gray drizzle of fear overcasts the present, which is still bright with promise.

God's Attitude toward Aging

So much for the human perspective on growing old. Let's see what God has to say about aging, first through a psalm of Moses and then through the life of Caleb.

A *Psalm of Moses*

Written by a senior citizen named Moses, Psalm 90 tells us about an eternal God, who existed before the mountains, who created the earth, and who, in fact, lives outside time itself (vv. 1–2). But unlike God, as Moses points out in the following verses, people have to deal with the temporal reality of aging.

> Thou dost turn man back into dust,
> And dost say, "Return, O children of men."
> For a thousand years in Thy sight

Are like yesterday when it passes by,
Or as a watch in the night.
Thou hast swept them away like a flood, they
fall asleep;
In the morning they are like grass which sprouts
anew.
In the morning it flourishes, and sprouts anew;
Toward evening it fades, and withers away. . . .
For all our days have declined in Thy fury;
We have finished our years like a sigh.
As for the days of our life, they contain seventy
years,
Or if due to strength, eighty years,
Yet their pride is but labor and sorrow;
For soon it is gone and we fly away.
(vv. 3–6, 9–10)

No wonder some people get discouraged about aging! This psalm sums up our lives on earth—we sprout, we wither, we die. But wait. The value of life isn't measured by the number of our years but by the quality of our days. The secret isn't in how long we live, but *how* we live. That's why Moses prays for the best use of his life, however long it may last.

So teach us to number our days,
That we may present to Thee a heart of wisdom.
(v. 12)

If we live wisely, we can approach old age with a song instead of a sigh.

O satisfy us in the morning with Thy
lovingkindness,
That we may sing for joy and be glad all our
days. (v. 14)

So the principle we derive from Psalm 90 is this: Since every day is a gift from God, live each one enthusiastically for Him.

The Life of Caleb

In Joshua 14, we find a man who embodies enthusiastic living. Israel has just conquered the Promised Land, and Joshua has begun to parcel out real estate to the individual tribes. Caleb, an eighty-five-year-old man, speaks up. His recollection of the past and his request for land reveal a lust for life that must have put the younger men to shame.

> Then the sons of Judah drew near to Joshua in Gilgal, and Caleb the son of Jephunneh the Kenizzite said to him, "You know the word which the Lord spoke to Moses the man of God concerning you and me in Kadesh-barnea. I was forty years old when Moses the servant of the Lord sent me from Kadesh-barnea to spy out the land, and I brought word back to him as it was in my heart. Nevertheless my brethren who went up with me made the heart of the people melt with fear; but I followed the Lord my God fully." (vv. 6–8)

Caleb's memory is sharp as ever. He remembers the day he, Joshua, and ten others were sent to spy out the land at Kadesh-barnea (Num. 13–14). Ten of the spies couldn't see beyond the giants and the fortified cities. Fear clouded their faith, and they forgot God's promises and power. Unfortunately, they infected the whole community of Israel with their fear.

Caleb and Joshua, however, viewed the situation through the lens of faith. They saw a land rich in fruit, flowing with milk and honey—the land God had promised them and would allow them to conquer. And Caleb hasn't forgotten God's promise to reward his faith.

> "So Moses swore on that day, saying, 'Surely the land on which your foot has trodden shall be an inheritance to you and to your children forever, because you have followed the Lord my God fully.'" (Josh. 14:9)

Notice, though, that Caleb isn't living in the past. He's ready to move ahead and start a new chapter of life—even as a senior citizen.

> "And now behold, the Lord has let me live, just as He spoke, these forty-five years, from the time that the Lord spoke this word to Moses, when Israel walked in the wilderness; and now behold, I am eighty-five years old today. I am still as strong today as I was in the day Moses sent me; as my strength

> was then, so my strength is now, for war and for going out and coming in. Now then, give me this hill country about which the Lord spoke on that day, for you heard on that day that Anakim were there, with great fortified cities; perhaps the Lord will be with me, and I shall drive them out as the Lord has spoken." (vv. 10–12)

Most of us, at eighty-five, would prefer some nice level ground where we could build a house with a screened-in porch and rocking chairs—especially after wandering around the wilderness for forty years with our cranky kinfolk! Not Caleb. "I'm as strong as ever! Give me the hill country," he says. "That's right. The tough terrain, the place where the giant Anakim live. The place everyone else is afraid of." Who could turn down such enthusiasm?

> So Joshua blessed him, and gave Hebron to Caleb the son of Jephunneh for an inheritance. Therefore, Hebron became the inheritance of Caleb the son of Jephunneh the Kenizzite until this day, because he followed the Lord God of Israel fully. (vv. 13–14)

Three lessons stand out from this remarkable man's life. First, it is possible for life's greatest achievements to take place in old age. Second, there is no such thing as retirement from our walk with God. And third, remaining vital and involved depends on our attitude. Douglas MacArthur said on his seventy-fifth birthday,

> In the central place of every heart there is a recording chamber; so long as it receives messages of beauty, hope, cheer, and courage, so long are you young. When the wires are all down and your heart is covered with the snows of pessimism and the ice of cynicism, then, and then only are you grown old.[1]

A New Attitude toward Aging

How did Caleb come to have such a robust attitude? "He followed the Lord God of Israel fully" (v. 14)—he had a vigorous

1. Douglas MacArthur, as quoted in *Quote Unquote*, comp. Lloyd Cory (Wheaton, Ill.: Scripture Press Publications, Victor Books, 1977), p. 15.

faith. Just because our skin wrinkles doesn't mean our walk with God has to shrivel up as well. Rather, our faith should increase with age as we look back on all God has done for us and look ahead to the great things He has yet to accomplish through us.

We may not be as physically robust as Caleb at eighty-five. But we can still follow his lead to the top of the mountain of faith and view life as a challenge instead of a threat. It's never too late, as Longfellow wrote:

> It is too late! Ah, nothing is too late
> Till the tired heart shall cease to palpitate.
> Cato learned Greek at eighty; Sophocles
> Wrote his grand Oedipus, and Simonides
> Bore off the prize of verse from his compeers,
> When each had numbered more than fourscore
> years,
> And Theophrastus, at fourscore and ten,
> Had but begun his "Characters of Men."
> Chaucer, at Woodstock with the nightingales,
> At sixty wrote the Canterbury Tales;
> Goethe at Weimar, toiling to the last,
> Completed Faust when eighty years were past. . . .
>
> What then? Shall we sit idly down and say
> The night hath come; it is no longer day?
> The night hath not yet come; we are not quite
> Cut off from labor by the failing light;
> Something remains for us to do or dare;
> Even the oldest tree some fruit may bear;
> Not Oedipus Coloneus, or Greek Ode,
> Or tales of pilgrims that one morning rode
> Out of the gateway of the Tabard Inn,
> But other something, would we but begin;
> For age is opportunity no less
> Than youth itself, though in another dress,
> And as the evening twilight fades away
> The sky is filled with stars, invisible by day.[2]

None of us can avoid aging; there is no fountain of youth. But

2. Henry Wadsworth Longfellow, excerpt from *Morituri Salutamus*, in *The Poetical Works of Longfellow* (Boston, Mass.: Houghton Mifflin Co., 1975), pp. 313–14.

there is a Fountain of Living Water. And thanks to Him, we can drink up all life has to offer—even in our old age.

Living Insights — STUDY ONE

Caleb had a hold on life and refused to let go. To him, old age was an adventure. For many people, old age is anything but a positive experience. The loss of a mate, a debilitating stroke or disease, or neglect by their families make many elderly yearn for the years gone by or look forward to the day the Lord calls them home.

Do you know anyone who needs a ray of hope in the darkness of old age? How can you provide some light? Perhaps you could help a retiree rediscover his usefulness by providing opportunities for using his gifts and abilities. Or how about taking advantage of someone's advice, capitalizing on her years of experience? Do you know a widow or widower with whom you could spend some time? Do you have parents or grandparents, aunts or uncles who wonder if they still occupy an important place in your life? Nursing homes are full of men and women whose families live far away or simply don't make an effort to visit. Showing an interest in older folks could make the difference between their giving up on life and still getting some enjoyment from it.

Whom can I encourage? ______________________________

____

How? ____

____

____

____

Living Insights — STUDY TWO

Just in case you think we stop making an impact when we get old, take a look at Paul's words to Titus.

> Older men are to be temperate, dignified, sensible, sound in faith, in love, in perseverance. Older

> women likewise are to be reverent in their behavior, not malicious gossips, nor enslaved to much wine, teaching what is good, that they may encourage the young women to love their husbands, to love their children, to be sensible, pure, workers at home, kind, being subject to their own husbands, that the word of God may not be dishonored. (Titus 2:2–5)

Paul reminded Titus that older people can have a dynamic ministry just by living godly lives. Never has that been more true than today. With families coming apart at the seams and leaders losing their grip on morality, younger folks are looking for assurance that the Christian life is worth living over the long haul. They want to know that it's possible to finish well, that the Christian faith is more than a fad or a political platform.

Older Christians can provide that assurance. People who have walked with God forty, fifty, sixty years know what it's like to stay in the race when they feel like quitting. They've seen God come through in a pinch time and time again. They've learned that love is more than a feeling; it's unwavering commitment. They've built families, raised children, lost loved ones, suffered with sickness, and come to grips with their own mortality. And they've learned that the only thing that never fails is Christ.

So, if you're getting on in years, remember, you ought to be in your prime spiritually—your opportunity to make an impact has never been greater. If, however, you have a way to go before your hair turns gray and you need some incentive to stay in the spiritual race, look around. Plenty of older runners would love to show you the way.

Chapter 9

STRENGTHENING YOUR GRIP ON PRAYER

Philippians 4:1–9; Matthew 6:5–15

Wait—don't turn that page! We promise this isn't your typical guilt-inducing, anxiety-producing, schedule-restricting message on prayer. We won't send someone to your home to peer over your shoulder, stopwatch in hand, while you have devotions. We won't ask you to duplicate the prayer life of some model saint from history. We won't even inspect your knees for calluses raised by long hours of prayer on hardwood floors.

No, our goal is to help you see prayer as a way to lighten your burdens, not add to them; to relieve anxiety, not increase it. The last thing we need to do is pour fuel on the fire of anxiety. We already have enough of that—from not quite being the people we really want to be, from not living the Christian life as abundantly as we'd hoped.

What Everyone Wants but Few of Us Have

In Philippians 4, Paul addresses a specific relational problem between two women in the church. In addition to his advice about this breach of fellowship, he promotes Christlike qualities all of us would like in our lives but few of us have.

> Therefore, my beloved brethren whom I long to see, my joy and crown, so *stand firm* in the Lord, my beloved.
>
> I urge Euodia and I urge Syntyche to *live in harmony* in the Lord. Indeed, true comrade, I ask you also to help these women who have shared my struggle in the cause of the gospel, together with Clement also, and the rest of my fellow workers, whose names are in the book of life.
>
> *Rejoice* in the Lord always; again I will say, rejoice! Let your *forbearing spirit* be known to all men. The Lord is near. . . .
>
> Finally, brethren, whatever is true, whatever is

> honorable, whatever is right, whatever is pure, whatever is lovely, whatever is of good repute, if there is any excellence and if anything worthy of praise, *let your mind dwell on these things*. The things you have learned and received and heard and seen in me, *practice these things;* and the God of peace shall be with you. (vv. 1–5, 8–9, emphasis added)

Stability . . . harmony . . . joy . . . patience . . . noble thoughts . . . consistency. What spiritually minded person wouldn't want such things? Yet because we don't achieve these in our lives, we become anxious. Add to our imperfect walk with God the unforeseen tragedies, temptations, and pressures that assault us, and our worry needle goes off the scale. Paul's answer to anxiety? Pray.

> Be anxious for nothing, but in everything by prayer and supplication with thanksgiving let your requests be made known to God. And the peace of God, which surpasses all comprehension, shall guard your hearts and your minds in Christ Jesus. (vv. 6–7)

What Went Wrong with Prayer

Pray. It sounds so simple. No complicated formula. No rigid schedule. No intricate instructions on recitation or posture. Just talk to God. So how did prayer get so complicated? History tells us that we have a tendency to take the simple things of God and repackage them in rigid religious formulas.

Why do we do this? Not because we don't believe in prayer, but precisely because we do—just as the Jews in Jesus' day did. William Barclay tells us that the rabbis used to say, "'Great is prayer, greater than all good works,'" and "'He who prays within his house surrounds it with a wall that is stronger than iron.' The only regret of the Rabbis was that it was not possible to pray all the day long."[1] For some, their seriousness about prayer turned into an unhealthy intensity, which bred impossibly high expectations, producing guilt and anxiety in the many who couldn't achieve them.

By the time Jesus stepped into this religious scene, prayer had degenerated in at least four ways.

1. William Barclay, *The Gospel of Matthew*, vol. 1, rev. ed., The Daily Study Bible Series (Philadelphia, Pa.: Westminster Press, 1975), p. 191.

It Had Become Formal and Ritualistic

There was little room for spontaneity in the Jewish system of prayer. Though some people recited prescribed liturgy with heartfelt devotion, most had fallen into a routine of checking prayer off the "to do" list. The Jews had specific prayers and creeds to be recited at specific times. The Shema, for example (which consisted of Deut. 6:4–9; 11:13–21; Num. 15:37–41), "had to be recited by every Jew every morning and every evening," before 9 A.M. and before 9 P.M.[2]

Besides doing this, the pious prayed three more times daily—9 A.M., noon, and 3 P.M.—regardless of where they were or what they were doing. Even their bodies had to adapt to the routine, as demonstrated by the proper stance for prayer—arms out, palms up, head bowed. In addition, Barclay explains,

> the Jewish liturgy supplied stated prayers for all occasions. There was hardly an event or a sight in life which had not its stated formula of prayer. There was prayer before and after each meal; there were prayers in connection with the light, the fire, the lightning, on seeing the new moon, comets, rain, tempest, at the sight of the sea, lakes, rivers, on receiving good news, on using new furniture, on entering or leaving a city. Everything had its prayer.[3]

It Had Become Long and Verbose

According to Barclay, one rabbi said, "'Whoever is long in prayer is heard.' . . . There was—and still is—a kind of subconscious idea that if men batter long enough at God's door, he will answer; that God can be talked, and even pestered, into condescension."[4] One popular prayer in Jesus' day even had sixteen adjectives in front of God's name! How different this practice was from Solomon's advice so many centuries before:

> Guard your steps as you go to the house of God, and draw near to listen rather than to offer the sacrifice of fools; for they do not know they are doing

2. Barclay, *The Gospel of Matthew*, p. 192.

3. Barclay, *The Gospel of Matthew*, pp. 193–94.

4. Barclay, *The Gospel of Matthew*, p. 195.

evil. Do not be hasty in word or impulsive in thought to bring up a matter in the presence of God. For God is in heaven and you are on the earth; therefore let your words be few. (Eccles. 5:1–2)

It Had Become Repetitious

Prayer became "a kind of intoxication with words."[5] Those who strove for piety lost themselves in hypnotic chants. Their emphasis had shifted from the message of prayer to the mechanics of it.

It Had Become Prideful

For the religious leaders of Jesus' day, prayer had become a glass case in which the glittering jewels of piety were displayed. Men were known to stop on the steps of the synagogue at appointed prayer times and dazzle onlookers with their lengthy prayers. As Barclay observed, "They were praying to men and not to God."[6]

As you can imagine, if people didn't conform to the "correct" style, they weren't considered to be truly devoted to God. Living up to others' expectations became the primary motivation to pray; and when that goal wasn't achieved, guilt imprisoned the person.

What Jesus Taught to Set Things Right

Into this rigid system of dos and don'ts came Jesus with His own instructions on prayer. Like a pebble in the highly polished shoe of Judaism, He irritated the self-impressed religious leaders. For He offered freedom from their chains of legalism, teaching that prayer was made for the ears of God, not the applause of men.

> "When you pray, you are not to be as the hypocrites; for they love to stand and pray in the synagogues and on the street corners, in order to be seen by men. Truly I say to you, they have their reward in full. But you, when you pray, go into your inner room, and when you have shut your door, pray to your Father who is in secret, and your Father who sees in secret will repay you." (Matt. 6:5–6)

5. Barclay, *The Gospel of Matthew*, pp. 196–97.

6. Barclay, *The Gospel of Matthew*, p. 197.

Don't misunderstand. Jesus isn't denigrating public prayer. He's simply warning us to *avoid hypocrisy*. The word *hypocrite* comes from an ancient Greek word meaning "one behind a mask." In Greek theater, actors changed roles by changing masks—each one representing a different character. Likewise, many public prayers resembled the masks of actors in a show. "They pray for approval," Jesus says, "and in the applause of the audience, they have their reward in full" (see v. 1). But an even greater reward awaits those whose prayers are motivated by relationship instead of recognition.

Jesus has a second warning about prayer: *Avoid meaningless repetition*.

> "And when you are praying, do not use meaningless repetition, as the Gentiles do, for they suppose that they will be heard for their many words." (v. 7)

Do you remember the Baal worshipers Elijah confronted on Mount Carmel? From morning until noon they droned on, "O Baal, answer us. O Baal, answer us" (see 1 Kings 18:26). And over in Acts 19:34, the Ephesians opposed the gospel by shouting, "Great is Artemis of the Ephesians!" for two hours straight. The Gentiles commonly rattled off chant-like praises to false gods for hours on end.

But before we get too smug, we should consider what Jesus would tell evangelical Christians today. He would probably put his warning like this: "Ditch the clichés." What do we mean when we say, "Lord, thank you for your many blessings"? What are we asking for when we say, "Be with brother Ed"? Are we merely repeating what we hear others say? What specifically are we thankful for? How exactly could God's presence encourage Ed? We shouldn't stop thanking God for our blessings or praying for brother Ed. But when we pray, we need to think about what we're saying and be natural. God isn't impressed with words; He wants to hear what's on our hearts.

We may not be moved by a new believer's simple "Hey, God, remember me?" But God is.

Finally, Jesus warns us to *forgive others*.

> "For if you forgive men for their transgressions, your heavenly Father will also forgive you. But if you do not forgive men, then your Father will not forgive your transgressions." (Matt. 6:14–15)

Did you know our prayer life can be affected by how we relate to others? Withholding forgiveness, harboring grudges, letting relational wounds fester—these can all get in the way of a healthy prayer life, even hinder our walk with God (see also 5:23–24; 1 John 4:20–21).

Pray to be heard by God, not applauded by people. Pray from the heart, not with meaningless repetition. And forgive others before approaching God. Pretty simple instructions. If followed, though, they will yield supernatural results. We'll be more aware of relationships that need mending. We'll draw closer to God. And He'll seem more like a loving Father and less like a drill sergeant.

What Prayer Changes

In the therapy of telling God everything, as a child confides in a loving parent, our circumstances may not change—but we will. We let Him carry the loads that are too heavy for us to bear. We trust Him to handle the problems that are out of our control. And our anxiety lessens as we learn to trust in His care.

In the last part of Matthew 6, Jesus reminds us that everything we need comes from our Father in heaven.

> "For this reason I say to you, do not be anxious for your life, as to what you shall eat, or what you shall drink; nor for your body, as to what you shall put on. Is not life more than food, and the body than clothing? Look at the birds of the air, that they do not sow, neither do they reap, nor gather into barns, and yet your heavenly Father feeds them. Are you not worth much more than they? And which of you by being anxious can add a single cubit to his life's span? And why are you anxious about clothing? Observe how the lilies of the field grow; they do not toil nor do they spin, yet I say to you that even Solomon in all his glory did not clothe himself like one of these. But if God so arrays the grass of the field, which is alive today and tomorrow is thrown into the furnace, will He not much more do so for you, O men of little faith? Do not be anxious then, saying, 'What shall we eat?' or 'What shall we drink?' or 'With what shall we clothe ourselves?' For all these things the Gentiles eagerly seek; for your heavenly Father knows that you need all these things. But seek first His kingdom and His righteousness; and all these things shall be added to you. Therefore do not be anxious for tomorrow; for tomorrow will

> care for itself. Each day has enough trouble of its own." (vv. 25–34)

Why should we be anxious, when our lives are in the care of a God who pays such close attention to birds and flowers? How much more must He care for us?

> God won't ignore us.
> God won't rip us off.
> God won't slap our hands.
> *We're His children.*

When we pray, we affirm that everything we need comes from His hand.

A Concluding Thought

Do you still feel a little anxious about talking with God? Let the words of Charles Spurgeon remind you of God's graciousness and rinse away any guilt or fear you may feel about your prayer life.

> If in prayer I come before a throne of grace, then the faults of my prayer will be overlooked. In beginning to pray, dear friends, you feel as if you did not pray. The groanings of your spirit when you rise from your knees are such that you think there is nothing in them. What a blotted, blurred, smeared prayer is it. Never mind; you have not come to the throne of justice. Otherwise, when God perceived the fault in the prayer He would spurn it—your broken words, your gaspings, and your stammerings are before a throne of grace.
>
> Our condescending King does not maintain a stately etiquette in his court like that which has been observed by princes among men, where a little mistake or a flaw would secure the petitioner's being dismissed with disgrace. Oh, no, the faulty cries of His children are not severely criticized by Him. The Lord High Chamberlain of the palace above, our Lord Jesus Christ, takes care to alter and amend every prayer before He presents it, and He makes the prayer perfect with His perfection and prevalent with His own merits. God looks upon the prayer as

presented through Christ and forgives all its own inherent faultiness.

How this ought to encourage any of us who feel ourselves to be feeble, wandering, and unskillful in prayer. If you cannot plead with God as sometimes you did in years gone by, if you feel as if somehow or other you had grown rusty in the work of supplication, never give up, but come still, yes and come oftener, for it is not a throne of severe criticism, but to a throne of grace you come.[7]

Grace, not guilt, is our reason to pray.

Living Insights STUDY ONE

You probably noticed that we skipped over the Lord's Prayer, which appears in Matthew 6:9–13. That's because, for many of us, these words of Christ have become so familiar that we often rattle them off without considering what they say about God . . . and us. We often see them as an obligatory part of a church service instead of a pattern for heartfelt prayer.

Take some time to read through verses 9 through 13 of Matthew 6—perhaps in an unfamiliar translation. Don't rush; let it sink in. Then respond to the following questions.

Do you think Jesus intended us to recite this prayer in public worship or to use it as a pattern for all prayer? Or could it be used for both?

What does verse 9 tell us about how we're related to God?

7. C. H. Spurgeon, "The Throne of Grace," from *Classic Sermons on Prayer*, comp. Warren W. Wiersbe (Grand Rapids, Mich.: Kregel Publications, 1987), p. 34.

What does that say about His readiness to hear our prayers and meet our needs? Feel free to draw on your own experience with your father or as a father (see also Matt. 7:7–11).

Do you relate to God as your loving Father? If not, how do you see Him?

What does Matthew 6:10 tell us about what we should pray for?

What do verses 11–13 tell us about what we should include in our prayers?

Take a moment to think about your own prayer life. Does it reflect a balance of making requests and giving God honor and praise?

Living Insights STUDY TWO

Using the Lord's Prayer as a guide, spend some time in prayer. Perhaps you'd like to try writing down your prayer, which not only enhances concentration but gives you a record of your conversation with God. You might even want to keep a separate prayer journal, to which you could come for spiritual refreshment and a reminder of God's faithfulness.

Chapter 10

STRENGTHENING YOUR GRIP ON LEISURE

Genesis 1–3

In his poignant essay "Life without Principle," Henry David Thoreau writes:

> If a man walk in the woods for love of them half of each day, he is in danger of being regarded as a loafer; but if he spends his whole day as a speculator, shearing off those woods and making earth bald before her time, he is esteemed an industrious and enterprising citizen. As if a town had no interest in its forests but to cut them down![1]

Thought-provoking, isn't it? And when applied to the spiritual realm, downright convicting. We have been sold a bill of goods that the committed Christian is the busy Christian—busy with people, busy with programs, busy with producing.

Because many Christians relentlessly drive themselves to be productive, they often view those who enjoy regular leisure time as undisciplined or irresponsible. We've been programmed to believe that fatigue is next to godliness, that it's better to burn out than to rust out. But either way, we're "out." Which means we can't finish the race God has set before us.

Now, don't get us wrong. We're not promoting a perpetual playtime. You won't hear us denouncing hard work, just overwork. We're not encouraging laziness, but leisure. There's a difference.

If your work has become your all-consuming interest or your greatest source of identity, worth, and security, then this chapter is for you. Though it may feel unnatural, sit back, put your feet up, and make yourself comfortable. Allow yourself the time to get a grip on leisure.

1. Henry David Thoreau, "Life without Principle," *Thoreau: Walden and Other Writings*, ed. Joseph Wood Krutch (New York, N.Y.: Bantam Books, 1962), p. 356.

The Place to Start: God

A scarcity of leisure in our lives reflects a lack of balance, with the scales tipped heavily toward work. The Scriptures, though, provide some help on how to restore that balance.

> Therefore be imitators of God, as beloved children. (Eph. 5:1)

The phrase *be imitators* is translated from the Greek word *mimeomai*, from which we get our word *mimic*. One scholar says the word "is always used in exhortations, and always in the continuous tense, suggesting a constant habit or practice."[2]

In Ephesians 5, Paul is exhorting believers to continually and consistently mimic God by loving others and living pure lives. Part of that godly lifestyle, he says, is the wise use of time (v. 16). And who uses time more wisely than God? Believe it or not, even the Creator of the universe took time for leisure (Gen. 2:1–3). So if we're going to imitate God, we need to include leisure time in our schedules.

Knowing God and imitating Him require a stillness, a slowing down, a quieting of our spirits. As the psalmist wrote, "Be still, and know that I am God" (Ps. 46:10a KJV). That's hard to do when work piles up, deadlines encroach, and responsibility weighs heavy on our shoulders. Yet look at the example of Jesus. He carried the weight of the whole world, but He still took time for solitude, away from His work (see Matt. 14:23; Luke 6:12).

Interestingly, the word *leisure* comes from the Latin word *licere*, which means "to be permitted." We must give ourselves permission for leisure if we're ever going to make it a vital part of our lives. We need to tell ourselves, "Hey, it's OK to take a break."

Still not convinced that leisure is a godly trait? Let's go back, then, to the Creation account, where we'll not only see how God blended leisure with work, but we'll learn how to use leisure time to honor God.

Four Guidelines from Genesis

The first three chapters of Genesis show us that leisure should have room for creativity, communication, rest, and relationships.

2. W. E. Vine, Merrill F. Unger, and William White, Jr., *An Expository Dictionary of Biblical Words*, (Nashville, Tenn.: Thomas Nelson Publishers, 1984), p. 578.

Creativity

"In the beginning," Genesis 1:1 tells us, "God created the heavens and the earth." From the "formless and void" (v. 2), He crafted beauty, order, and purpose. Teal-colored oceans gilded with sunlight and teeming with sea creatures. Powder blue skies streaked with clouds and swirling with busy birds. Stars sprayed across the canvas of night. The intricate human body and brain. All of these were conceived in God's mind and fashioned through His fingertips.

If we are to mimic God, we must also take time to create. When we write, compose, make music, dance, paint, sculpt, build, sew, bake, or solve problems, we reflect the creativity of our God. The ability to create sets us apart from the animal kingdom and confirms that we are made in His image.

Communication

Further on in Genesis 1, we see that God is a communicator as well as Creator. Even before He crafted Adam, communication existed among the members of the Godhead.

> Then God said, "Let Us make man in Our image, according to Our likeness; and let them rule over the fish of the sea and over the birds of the sky and over the cattle and over all the earth, and over every creeping thing that creeps on the earth." (v. 26)

And after creating Adam and Eve, God communicated with them.

> And God created man in His own image, in the image of God He created him; male and female He created them. And God blessed them; and God said to them, "Be fruitful and multiply, and fill the earth, and subdue it; and rule over the fish of the sea and over the birds of the sky, and over every living thing that moves on the earth." Then God said, "Behold, I have given you every plant yielding seed that is on the surface of all the earth, and every tree which has fruit yielding seed; it shall be food for you; and to every beast of the earth and to every bird of the sky and to every thing that moves on the earth which has life, I have given every green plant for food"; and it was so. And God saw all that He had made, and behold, it was very good. (vv. 27–31a)

God is an expressive being—not merely some abstract force of nature. He is a God who sees, who hears, who feels, and who speaks. So, too, are we to communicate . . . to share, to listen, to care, to think . . . to get to know God, ourselves, and others. This type of communication is part of a balanced life.

Rest

On the seventh day, God created . . . the weekend!

> Thus the heavens and the earth were completed, and all their hosts. And by the seventh day God completed His work which He had done; and He rested on the seventh day from all His work which He had done. Then God blessed the seventh day and sanctified it, because in it He rested from all His work which God had created and made. (2:1–3)

God deliberately stopped working, not because He ran out of ideas or energy—omnipotence never gets tired. No, He stopped to enjoy His creation. He made rest a priority, giving us a pattern to follow.

How about you? Are you resting? Do you take time to set your work aside and reflect? Careful now. We're not talking about sinking into the couch with the remote control in one hand and a Big Gulp in the other. We're talking about restful contemplation, thanking God for what He has allowed you to accomplish, reflecting on His goodness and grace. This kind of rest, though often perceived by the overly busy as a waste of time, is anything but that, as one poet observed:

> I wasted an hour one morning beside a mountain
> stream,
> I seized a cloud from the sky above and fashioned
> myself a dream,
> In the hush of the early twilight, far from the
> haunts of men,
> I wasted a summer evening, and fashioned my
> dream again.
> Wasted? Perhaps. Folks say so who never have
> walked with God,
> When lanes are purple with lilacs or yellow with
> goldenrod.
> But I have found strength for my labors in that

one short evening hour.
I have found joy and contentment; I have found
peace and power.
My dreaming has left me a treasure, a hope that is
strong and true.
From wasted hours I have built my life and found
my faith anew.[3]

You might be amazed at how a little rest can bring you closer to your Heavenly Father. The Lord, my Shepherd, "makes me lie down in green pastures; He leads me beside quiet waters. He restores my soul" (Ps. 23:2–3a).

Relationships

Something else leisure does for us is give us time to build relationships. Again, God is our model. Not only did He consistently spend time with Adam and Eve (Gen. 3:8a), but He paid attention to their hearts and could therefore anticipate their needs. Look at how God knew that Adam needed Eve before Adam knew it himself.

> And the Lord God planted a garden toward the east, in Eden; and there He placed the man whom He had formed. And out of the ground the Lord God caused to grow every tree that is pleasing to the sight and good for food; the tree of life also in the midst of the garden, and the tree of the knowledge of good and evil. . . . Then the Lord God said, "It is not good for the man to be alone; I will make him a helper suitable for him." . . . So the Lord God caused a deep sleep to fall upon the man, and he slept; then He took one of his ribs, and closed up the flesh at that place. And the Lord God fashioned into a woman the rib which He had taken from the man, and brought her to the man. (Gen. 2:8–9, 18, 21–22)

Adam never had to say, "Excuse me, God, but I'm really lonesome in the garden by myself." God saw it first and responded to the need.

Relating to others involves more than verbal communication; it means catching the twinkle in an eye, a certain set of the jaw,

3. Author unknown.

or a slumping of the shoulders. It means reading a person's nonverbal language. When we're in touch with someone, we hear the words and feelings that aren't said.

Are you cultivating relationships as part of your leisure activities? They take time and effort and attention. Which means leisure has to be more than just solitude or entertainment. It must include time to talk, listen, laugh, comfort, encourage, and confront.

How to Implement Leisure

Leisure helps develop in us the capacity to perceive the eternal. It provides the time to get recentered in God, to recall what matters most in life. Without leisure, we lose our way.

To strengthen your grip on leisure, hold on to these two pieces of advice. First: *Deliberately stop being absorbed by worries*. You know what we worry about most? Nonessentials, unchangeables, and impossibles. It's time we take to heart the words of Jesus in Matthew 6 and decide not to allow worry to rob us of God's peace (see vv. 25–34).

Second: *Consciously take time for leisure*. Change your routine. Plan fun into your schedule. Stop and smell a few flowers, listen to a bird or two, and let the sunset sink into your soul. Talk to your friends and family about something besides the weather. Then you'll not only know what leisure is, you'll be reflecting some of the very qualities of God.

Living Insights STUDY ONE

How about taking some leisure time now. Let these words from Orin L. Crane wash over your weary bones and saturate your spirit with the joy that comes from truly resting in the Lord.

> Slow me down, Lord.
>
> Ease the pounding of my heart by the quieting of my mind.
>
> Steady my hurried pace with a vision of the eternal reach of time.
>
> Give me, amid the confusion of the day, the calmness of the everlasting hills.
>
> Break the tensions of my nerves and muscles with the soothing music of the singing streams that live in my memory.

Teach me the art of taking minute vacations—of slowing down to look at a flower, to chat with a friend, to pat a dog, to smile at a child, to read a few lines from a good book.

Slow me down, Lord, and inspire me to send my roots deep into the soil of life's enduring values, that I may grow toward my greater destiny.

Remind me each day that the race is not always to the swift; that there is more to life than increasing its speed.

Let me look upward to the towering oak and know that it grew great and strong because it grew slowly and well.[4]

Living Insights — STUDY TWO

"I always wanted to learn to play the guitar."

"I wish I could just sit and absorb some great classical music."

"It seems like everything I read has to do with my profession. I haven't read a good biography or novel in years."

"I'd love to write about my experiences, but I can't seem to find the time."

"I'm sorry, honey. I know I said we would go to the art museum, but there's so much that needs to be done around the house."

Sound familiar? Most of us have discovered that, if we don't plan to take some leisure time, it won't happen.

Stop right now and block out some time in your schedule to do something you've been wanting to do for a long while. Give that guitar teacher a call; see what's involved with taking lessons. Instead of the usual movie, shuttle your family to the symphony or "Shakespeare in the Park." You probably have a museum or two in your community that you didn't even know existed. Check it out.

Take an afternoon to browse the library or a bookstore, and pick up a book that has nothing to do with your profession—an

4. Orin L. Crane, "Slow Me Down, Lord," from *Treasury of the Familiar*, Ralph Woods, ed. The MacMillan, Co., 1970.

exhilarating science fiction novel, a collection of poetry, an anthology of *Far Side* cartoons. And, oh yes, be sure you allow some time to read it.

Go camping. Stand on a craggy cliff overlooking a lake, and take a long sip of the cool morning air.

Start keeping a journal of your life experiences—just take fifteen minutes, three nights a week, to record your thoughts. You may find that you really enjoy writing and want to do more.

These are just a few suggestions. Choose one and do it, or at least plan it, this week. Fill in the following pledge to keep yourself accountable.

I promise to ____

____

____

by this time next week.

____

signature

Chapter 11

STRENGTHENING YOUR GRIP ON MISSIONS

Isaiah 6:1–12

Sandy, moved by the missionary's presentation, filled out her commitment card and slipped it between the pages of her Bible. As soon as the service ended, she would drop it in the box at the back of the church. In the meantime, she sat quietly, thinking about the projected images of children flocking around a teacher to hear their first Bible story. Of tribal people with their hands raised in worship. Of a group of men, who had once prayed to animal spirits, now sitting with heads bowed, approaching the throne of Jehovah.

I can be a part of that, she thought. *I can make an impact. I can proclaim the gospel. Sign me up! The world is waiting!* . . .

Is that all there is to missions? See a slide show, then save the world? Though Sandy's enthusiasm is admirable, she might be forgetting that missions involves more than proclamation. It requires preparation.

Before we take the Living Water to the world, it must first seep into our own souls. Only then, Isaiah 6 teaches us, are we ready for missions.

Relevant Principles from an Ancient Prophet

Twenty-seven centuries ago, God got Isaiah's attention in the wake of King Uzziah's death. Uzziah was one of the few righteous rulers to occupy the throne of Judah, reigning for a mostly golden fifty-two years. Later in life, though, his character tarnished as he came to personify the nation's attitude of pride and self-sufficiency. In his arrogance, he entered the temple to burn incense—a duty reserved solely for the priests. God struck him with leprosy for this presumptuous sin, and he remained a leper until he died.

Isaiah and Uzziah may have known one another fairly well, especially if Isaiah was descended from aristocracy.[1] He may even

1. "Because of his ready access to the court and his seeming lack of inhibition in confronting monarchs (cf. chs. 7, 36–39), scholars have often suggested that Isaiah was of noble, if not royal, descent." *The Eerdmans Bible Dictionary*, ed. Allen C. Myers (Grand Rapids, Mich.: William B. Eerdmans Publishing Co., 1987), p. 531.

have been related to the king.[2] We do know that Isaiah authored a biography of Uzziah (see 2 Chron. 26:22).

The passing of Uzziah's era must have shaken Isaiah. The king the nation had taken for granted was gone—who would guide Judah's future now? Someone corrupt, or someone godly? At this vulnerable moment of personal and national mourning, God gave Isaiah a glimpse of the heavenly King and a heart to speak for Him.

From Isaiah's vision we can draw five principles that will prepare us for reaching the world for Christ.

God Uses Circumstances to Make Us Aware of His Presence

> In the year of King Uzziah's death, I saw the Lord sitting on a throne, lofty and exalted, with the train of His robe filling the temple. (Isa. 6:1)

In this verse, the juxtaposition of Uzziah's death with Isaiah's vision of God may be more than a time indicator. It suggests that God broke into Isaiah's grief with a vision of His splendor, reminding him that God doesn't wring His hands or pace across heaven's carpet when He hears about someone's death. Rather, God sits calmly on the throne—the symbol of His authority, of His absolute control—waiting for just the right moment to reveal Himself.

Sometimes, as with Isaiah, the death of a friend drives us to God. Other times, it's the loss of a job, a crippling illness, a sudden move, a child's injury. Whatever the circumstances, God can penetrate our darkness with His light. When we have basked in His presence and sensed His comfort, we realize we don't have to go it alone. Then we are ready to take the comfort of the Lord to others who need His healing touch.

God Reveals His Character to Make Us See Our Need

Something about standing before God helps us see our neediness. During his vision, Isaiah's need came to light before the brilliance of God's glory.

> Seraphim stood above Him, each having six wings; with two he covered his face, and with two he covered

2. Isaiah 1:1 says that Isaiah was "the son of Amoz," who, according to Herbert Lockyer, "some scholars suggest . . . was the uncle of Uzziah which, if true, would make Isaiah the king's cousin." *All the Men of the Bible* (Grand Rapids, Mich.: Zondervan Publishing House, 1958), p. 157.

> his feet, and with two he flew. And one called out to another and said,
>
> "Holy, Holy, Holy, is the Lord of hosts,
> The whole earth is full of His glory."
>
> And the foundations of the thresholds trembled at the voice of him who called out, while the temple was filling with smoke. (vv. 2–4)

Can you imagine what that was like?

> This celestial worship service literally rocked the foundations of the temple! In their antiphony of praise, the angels thundered, "Holy, Holy, Holy." . . . The Lord of hosts, they sing, is infinitely holy.[3]

At the display of such holiness, Isaiah's eyes suddenly turned to himself.

> Then I said,
> "Woe is me, for I am ruined!
> Because I am a man of unclean lips,
> And I live among a people of unclean lips;
> For my eyes have seen the King, the Lord of hosts." (v. 5)[4]

How else can one respond when confronted with God's holiness? We may think we're living a pretty good life, until our flaws show up under the radiance of His revealing light.

The Lord, however, didn't abandon Isaiah to his sinfulness.

> Then one of the seraphim flew to me, with a burning coal in his hand which he had taken from the altar with tongs. And he touched my mouth with it and said, "Behold, this has touched your lips; and your iniquity is taken away, and your sin is forgiven." (vv. 6–7)

3. As quoted from the study guide *Making New Discoveries*, coauthored by Gary Matlack, from the Bible-teaching ministry of Charles R. Swindoll (Anaheim, Calif.: Insight for Living, 1995), p. 31.

4. Isaiah, though greatly used by God, still had a sinful nature, as did the people to whom he ministered. Commentators generally agree that the prophet's admission of "unclean lips" signifies his awareness of his sinful nature in light of God's holiness. "Unclean lips," however, might also indicate that Isaiah struggled with a particular sin of the tongue, such as profanity, which he needed to confess to receive God's cleansing.

Isaiah, like all of us, needed hope that a sinful human could stand before a holy God without fear of judgment. So God touched him with the cleansing fire of forgiveness.

Notice that the seraph with the burning coal flew to Isaiah (v. 6). The Holy reached out to the hopeless. The Light delved into the darkness. What a picture of the forgiveness God provides for us in Christ.

> In the presence of the Lord, we are all unclean and even the fiery seraphim are not clean before Him or worthy to behold Him. How fortunate, however, that Christ as the Priestly King has not only an exalted *throne*, but also an *altar*, where sins can be burned away, as happened with this seer.[5]

Because of Jesus Christ, we can approach God without being consumed by His holiness. Just as God sent the angel to cleanse Isaiah's lips, He sent Christ to cleanse our sin and open the door to God's throne room.

What a missions training program! First we see God's holiness. Next we see our own sinfulness. Then we marvel that God doesn't hold it against us; rather, He burns our sins away with his searing light. Then, and only then, are we ready to tell others about the Lord's unfathomable mercy and grace.

God Gives Us Hope to Make Us Realize We Are Useful

God's plan went beyond the cleansing of Isaiah. The dialogue that follows reveals the Lord's heart for the lost and His desire to use us in reaching them.

> Then I heard the voice of the Lord, saying, "Whom shall I send, and who will go for Us?" Then I said, "Here am I. Send me!" (v. 8)

How gracious of God to include us in His plan to reach the lost and affirm our value and usefulness. He could have approached His people any way He wanted—with a chorus of angels or direct address from His throne. Yet He uses people just like you and me. He touches us, changes us, gives us hope. Then he sends us.

5. Harry Bultema, *Commentary on Isaiah*, trans. Cornelius Lambregtse (Grand Rapids, Mich.: Kregel Publications, 1981), p. 96.

God Expands Our Vision to Make Us Evaluate Our Availability

Did you notice that God *asked*, "Who will go?" God is sovereign, but He's no bully. He doesn't mug us, blindfold us, and drop us in the weeds of the mission field with a map to all the lost souls. He says, "This is where I'm going; will you go with me?"

Isaiah said, "Yes, I'll go; send me." Not out of blind obligation or religious duty, but because he was now looking at life through God's lens; he had caught God's vision for reaching the world.

God Tells Us the Truth to Make Us Focus on Reality

Before you say, "Oh, who wouldn't enlist after a vision like that," consider Isaiah's assignment.

> "Go, and tell this people:
> 'Keep on listening, but do not perceive;
> Keep on looking, but do not understand.'
> Render the hearts of this people insensitive,
> Their ears dull,
> And their eyes dim,
> Lest they see with their eyes,
> Hear with their ears,
> Understand with their hearts,
> And return and be healed."
> Then I said, "Lord, how long?" And He answered,
> "Until cities are devastated and without inhabitant,
> Houses are without people,
> And the land is utterly desolate,
> The Lord has removed men far away,
> And the forsaken places are many in the midst of
> the land." (vv. 9–12)

What a job description! "Isaiah, I want you to take My message to a people who will refuse to listen. And, by the way, I'll be bringing destruction on the nation soon."

God's plan never guarantees His messengers' success. He doesn't paint a rosy picture of instant, total, and grateful revival. He hands us reality. The center of God's will may not always be the calmest or safest place, as the crucifixion of Christ shows us. Nevertheless, participating in His plan brings a sense of satisfaction and fulfillment unattainable by pursuing personal ambitions.

Strengthening our grip on missions requires a firm handle on reality. When we reach out to others in the name of Christ, our greatest confirmation is not the tangible results of our labor. Rather, it's the inner assurance that we're in the nucleus of God's will.

And What about You and Me . . . Today?

F. B. Meyer writes:

> In some unlikely quarter, in a shepherd's hut, or in an [artisan's] cottage, God has his prepared and appointed instrument. As yet the shaft is hidden in his quiver, in the shadow of his hand; but at the precise moment at which it will tell with the greatest effect, it will be produced and launched on the air.[6]

Could you be that arrow? You never know. God may be waiting for just the right moment to pull you from the quiver and slip you onto His bowstring. He may not shoot you overseas or even across the country. Maybe He just wants to get you beyond your own backyard. But arrows must be sharpened before they're launched.

So proclaim. But don't forget to prepare.

Living Insights — STUDY ONE

How about taking some time to evaluate your feelings about missions? Don't worry, we're not asking you to pack up and move to Rwanda. No one will send your responses to your pastor or a mission board.

It might be enlightening for you, though, to examine your attitude about reaching the lost as part of God's overall plan. Depending on your responses, you might want to adjust your lifestyle to spend more time with non-Christians, give more to missions, write to your church's missionaries, or help train others to share their faith. Or you may want to simply respond to God with thanks and worship for reaching you through a missions-minded person. Here are some questions to kindle the fires of reflection.

When you hear the word *missions*, what comes to mind?

---

6. F. B. Meyer, *David: Shepherd Psalmist—King* (Grand Rapids, Mich.: Zondervan Publishing House, 1953), p. 11.

Does *missions* mean "overseas outreach," or can it apply to local evangelism (see Acts 1:8)?

Is missions the job of a select few, or does God expect all of us to participate at some level (see Matt. 28:18–20; Eph. 6:19)?

At what level are you currently involved with outreach? Going? Praying? Giving? Some other way?

Do you feel God calling you to take a specific action as a result of this exercise?

Living Insights — STUDY TWO

Isaiah's encounter teaches us that the best way to equip ourselves to feed the hungry souls of others is to first feast on the holiness of God. Then we will know the God whom we proclaim.

How well do we know God? Not what the pastor says about

Him. Not the missions program. Not religious lingo. But the very Person of God and the attributes He possesses? Is God's holiness just a theological concept to us? Or have we discovered, as R. C. Sproul did as a young college student, that God's holiness is meant to be more than a concept—it's a consuming reality.

> I was in a posture of prayer, but I had nothing to say. I knelt there quietly, allowing the sense of the presence of a holy God to fill me. The beat of my heart was telltale, a thump-thump against my chest. An icy chill started at the base of my spine and crept up my neck. Fear swept over me. I fought the impulse to run from the foreboding presence that gripped me.
>
> The terror passed, but soon it was followed by another wave. This wave was different. It was a flooding of my soul of unspeakable peace, a peace that brought instant rest and repose to my troubled spirit. At once I was comfortable. I wanted to linger there. To say nothing. To do nothing. Simply to bask in the presence of God. That moment was life transforming. Something deep in my spirit was being settled once for all. From this moment there could be no turning back; there could be no erasure of the indelible imprint of its power. I was alone with God. A holy God. An awesome God. A God who could fill me with terror in one second and with peace in the next. I knew in that hour that I had tasted of the Holy Grail.[7]

Once we get a glimpse of God like that, we're ready to turn in our commitment card. How about spending a little time on your knees right now, opening your spirit to a glimpse of the Almighty?

7. R. C. Sproul, *The Holiness of God* (Wheaton, Ill.: Tyndale House Publishers, 1985), p. 6.

Chapter 12

STRENGTHENING YOUR GRIP ON GODLINESS

1 Corinthians 10:1–13

I can't believe it; I'm actually here.

Steve had a picturesque view of the seminary campus from the parking lot across the street. The administration building, with its shadowed arches and rustic bell tower, presided over a lawn so spacious and green that it looked out of place in this inner-city neighborhood. The adjacent library, a larger and more contemporary structure, stood as a monument to the school's growth and success over its ninety-six-year history.

Setting his briefcase on the sidewalk, Steve stuffed his hands in his pockets and let it all soak in. He debated whether to slip off his shoes before walking onto holy ground. And for a moment, he thought he heard the voices of angels. But it was just the wind singing through the trees and apartment buildings along Old Cedar Street.

He glanced at his watch—*Can't be late for my first day of class.* Then he grabbed the briefcase and started across the street toward the campus . . . **where God lived.**

Halfway through the semester, Steve wondered if God had relocated to the suburbs. Seminary seemed more like a slippery slope than holy ground. He had encountered no burning bush, but his candle was lit at both ends and melting fast—Greek vocabulary to memorize, theology papers to write, lessons to prepare for the singles group, and a family to feed. His prayer life, except for occasional "flare prayers" of "HELP!" and "WHAT AM I DOING HERE?" was nonexistent. Somehow, in this oasis of living water, Steve's spiritual palate had grown dry as dust.

Anybody Seen God Lately?

Amazing, isn't it? A seminary, especially one with a strong evangelical tradition, is the last place we would expect to find someone struggling to connect with God. But it happens, and not just in seminaries. People smack-dab in the middle of Christian organizations sometimes miss God. Pastors and parishioners of churches. Administrators in parachurch ministries. Children in Christian homes. Students in Christian schools.

In fact, it's easier than you may think to lose our sensitivity toward God in a Christian environment. When we're around His people regularly, talking His language, watching Him work, enjoying His blessings, we can start to take Him for granted. In short, we can loosen our grip on God while we're handling all the things that pertain to Him.

Israel: So Much of God, So Little Godliness

This problem is nothing new. Who had more of God than the Israelites in Moses' day? They were a people selected by grace to be God's own . . . freed from Egypt's chains . . . rescued from Pharaoh's army . . . sustained by God's miraculous provision in the wilderness. But they were ungrateful, hardened, faithless. As cold and dark toward God as charred sticks in a doused campfire. The Great Deliverer, in their eyes, had become a cruel taskmaster.

In Paul's day, the Corinthians also managed to miss God. The apostle tried to convince them that there's more to spiritual growth than simply being exposed to God; that maturity requires self-discipline and consistency (see 1 Cor. 9:24–27). In 1 Corinthians 10, he cites Israel as proof that privilege doesn't guarantee piety.

> For I do not want you to be unaware, brethren, that our fathers were all under the cloud, and all passed through the sea; and all were baptized into Moses in the cloud and in the sea; and all ate the same spiritual food; and all drank the same spiritual drink, for they were drinking from a spiritual rock which followed them; and the rock was Christ. (vv. 1–4)

The Israelites had no reason to cry, "Oh, God, if You would only show Yourself." His presence was all around them. He gave them Moses to lead them out of bondage and guide them through the wilderness. He showed them the way with the cloud and the pillar of fire. He cleaved the sea apart so they could escape the wrath of Pharaoh. He made rocks gush water and covered the barren wilderness with bread. And though they may not have known it at the time, the preincarnate Christ accompanied them every step of their journey.

But notice what happened to them:

> Nevertheless, with most of them God was not well-pleased; for they were laid low in the wilderness. (v. 5)

What a contrast to verses 1–4! Loaded high with blessings . . . laid low in the wilderness. That's another way of saying they were "strewn all over the desert."[1] Commentator David Lowery sheds light on the lesson Paul wanted to drive home to the Corinthians.

> The presence of supernatural privileges in the lives of Old Testament Israelites did not produce automatic success. On the contrary, in spite of their special advantages, most of them (in fact, all but two members of one generation, Joshua and Caleb) experienced God's discipline, were disqualified, and died in the desert (Num. 14:29). In light of this, Paul's avowed need for personal self-discipline (1 Cor. 9:27) was genuine since even Moses was disqualified for the prize (Num. 20:12).[2]

Guess what? The same thing can happen to us. We can disqualify ourselves from future blessings and wander around in a spiritual wilderness. We can miss God right in the middle of church, the mission field, and the Christian home. Scary thought. But, according to Paul, it doesn't have to come true.

> Now these things happened as examples for us. (1 Cor. 10:6a; see also v. 11)

We can learn from the Israelites' mistakes. Let's continue, then, in Paul's letter to find out how the Israelites slid into such a condition. And let's determine, with God's help, to avoid the same pitfalls.

1. Gordon D. Fee, *The First Epistle to the Corinthians*, in The New International Commentary on the New Testament Series (1987; reprint, Grand Rapids, Mich.: William B. Eerdmans Publishing Co., 1988), p. 450.

2. David K. Lowery, "1 Corinthians," in *The Bible Knowledge Commentary*, New Testament edition, ed. John F. Walvoord and Roy B. Zuck (Wheaton, Ill.: Scripture Press Publications, Victor Books, 1983), p. 526.

Five Perilous Circles

How did the Israelites bring such tragedy on themselves? It didn't happen overnight, but gradually. They swam into a swirling vortex of destruction by taking one disobedient stroke at a time—like passing through a series of concentric circles, one after another, until the suction pulled them under.

Circle One: Craving Evil Things

> Now these things happened as examples for us, that we should not crave evil things, as they also craved. (v. 6; compare Num. 11:4, 34)

This is the outer rim of the funnel that began to pull the Israelites away from God. They knew they should follow Him, but they followed their appetites instead. When the going got tough, they gossiped against Moses, stopped trusting God, and longed for the security of their former captivity.

How foolish. How faithless. How very much like us. We have our outer circles of sin too, don't we? The pressure is often so slight that we don't feel it. We become dissatisfied with something in our lives. Then we begin to wonder, then fantasize, then experiment, then . . .

Circle Two: Idolatry

> And do not be idolaters, as some of them were; as it is written, "The people sat down to eat and drink, and stood up to play." (1 Cor. 10:7; compare Exod. 32:1–20)

When we put something besides God on the throne of our lives—self, sex, money, power, fame, food—it becomes idolatry. The shift may be subtle, almost indiscernible. Nobody ever stands up and announces, "I now have a new idol." Idols begin by tugging at our attention. Then they slurp up our time, our devotion, and eventually our worship.

Oh, we may not sculpt a golden calf, as the Israelites did. But our idols are just as real. And they can lead us in only one direction—away from God.

Circle Three: Immorality

> Nor let us act immorally, as some of them did, and

> twenty-three thousand fell in one day.[3] (1 Cor. 10:8; compare Num. 25:1–9)

Paul had good reason to command the Corinthians to avoid immorality, as Horst Reisser explains:

> In the Pauline writings the word-group *porne* denotes any kind of illegitimate sexual intercourse. Paul's usage of the word-group predominantly in 1 Cor. (14 times) shows that the problem was posed for him in an acute way in this church. Corinth was a town with traditional temple prostitution. . . . As an important port it was especially open to the syncretism of the ancient world and stamped with sexual licentiousness in the slums around the harbour and in the sanctuaries. But it was from the circles of this harbour proletariat that many members of the Corinthian Church came.[4]

The Israelites, too, included pagan sex rituals among their offenses against God (see Num. 25:1–4). Sexual sin—pornography, adultery, homosexuality—is tough to break free from once it takes hold. Israel, and Corinth, serve as grim reminders of what can happen if we get carried away by the current of sexual sin.

Circle Four: Presuming upon God

> Nor let us try the Lord, as some of them did, and were destroyed by the serpents. (1 Cor. 10:9; compare Num. 21:4–6)

The Israelites' perspective was so distorted by sin that they accused God of carrying out an evil plan instead of a good one. "Why have you brought us up out of Egypt to die in the wilderness?" they asked God and Moses (v. 5). How arrogant, after all God had done for them.

3. Numbers 25:9 gives the figure as twenty-four thousand. How do we account for this apparent discrepancy between Moses and Paul? Gleason L. Archer argues that Paul is not referring to Numbers 25 but Exodus 32:35, based on his having quoted 32:6 in 1 Corinthians 10:7. Archer says Paul supplies the number that Moses omitted. *Encyclopedia of Bible Difficulties* (Grand Rapids, Mich.: Zondervan Publishing House, Regency Reference Library, 1982), p. 141. Others speculate that Paul may have intended to include only those who fell "in one day." A third option is a possible scribal error in the copying of the text.

4. *The New International Dictionary of New Testament Theology*, gen. ed. Colin Brown (Grand Rapids, Mich.: Zondervan Publishing House, Regency Reference Library, 1986), vol. 1, p. 500.

Yet we do the same thing. When the dust of difficulty clouds our eternal perspective, how often do we say, "God, why are you doing this to me?" His plans for us are always good, even when they include adversity (see Rom. 8:28–30). When we presume upon God and accuse Him of abusing us, we risk drifting even further away from Him.

Circle Five: Grumbling

> Nor grumble, as some of them did, and were destroyed by the destroyer. (1 Cor. 10:10; compare Num. 16:41–50)

God didn't judge the Israelites for merely mumbling idle complaints under their breath. They were heaping blame on Moses and Aaron for their difficulties (see v. 41). They were despising the very ones God had chosen to lead them out of cruel bondage.

When we're far from God, we tend to blame Him and those who speak for Him for our troubles. God's desire, however, is for our difficulties to lead us straight to Him.

Notice the progression of the five circles. The Israelites began to crave evil, trying to satisfy themselves with everything but God. This led them to worship other gods. With Jehovah off the throne, nothing was taboo—not even gross immorality. And since God was no longer the object of their worship, they could only presume upon Him and grumble against Him.

Common Reactions to This Instruction

How easily we look at the failures of others and say, "That'll never happen to me." Paul faces that idea straight on too:

> Therefore let him who thinks he stands take heed lest he fall. (1 Cor. 10:12)

It *can* happen to us, and it often does. We Christians, who possess even more blessings than the Old Testament Israelites, can become jaded. We can take God for granted. And when He gets too familiar, too comfortable, too "everyday," we can forget He's even there.

Another response is equally dangerous. We can identify so closely with Israel that we feel hopeless, convinced that giving in to sin is our best option. "Don't do it," says Paul.

> No temptation has overtaken you but such as is common to man; and God is faithful, who will not allow you to be tempted beyond what you are able, but with the temptation will provide the way of escape also, that you may be able to endure it. (v. 13)

God knows our limits even better than we do. And He doesn't entice us to sin (James 1:13)—He rescues us from it. When resisting seems futile, He helps us not only survive temptation but honor Him through it.

Crucial Questions for Application

Let's rejoin our disillusioned seminary student. Four reflective questions will help put him, and us, back in touch with God.

1. Have you lost your delight in the Lord? Are spiritual things tasting a little dry lately? Maybe you're craving something you shouldn't.
2. Have you stopped taking God seriously? Are you tolerating things in your life that you didn't, say, five or ten years ago? Who's on the throne of your life? Who's ruling over your passions? Do you detect any areas of erosion in your values?
3. Do you realize that you could wander in the wilderness for years if nothing changes? Is the danger you're in real to you?
4. Finally, are you willing to confess the deadness of your spirituality to the Lord and to others and let them help revive it?

Remember, we serve a risen Savior. So there's no such thing as dead Christianity. He lives—in church, at home, at work, in ministry . . . even in Greek class.

Living Insights STUDY ONE

Admit it, now. You've had some experience with grumbling. You've thought, during one of those wilderness treks, that Romans 8:28 should read something like this: "And we know that God causes all things to work together for good to those who love God, to those who are called according to His purpose . . . that is, unless He's mad at me. Or doesn't feel like it. Or comes across something He can't quite handle."

The truth is, God *rejoices* in doing us good. That doesn't mean the Christian life is always easy; far from it. But God works even adversity for our good.

Skeptical? Listen to the words of John Piper:

> Can you imagine what it would be like to hear God singing?
>
> A mere *spoken* word from his mouth brought the universe into existence. What would happen if God lifted up his voice and not only spoke but sang! Perhaps a new heaven and a new earth would be created. . . .
>
> What do you hear when you imagine the voice of God singing?
>
> I hear the booming of Niagara Falls mingled with the trickle of a mossy mountain stream. I hear the blast of Mt. St. Helens mingled with a kitten's purr. I hear the power of an East Coast hurricane and the barely audible puff of a night snow in the woods. And I hear the unimaginable roar of the sun, 865,000 miles thick, 1,300,000 times bigger than the earth, and nothing but fire, 1,000,000 degrees centigrade on the cooler surface of the corona. But I hear this unimaginable roar mingled with the tender, warm crackling of logs in the living room on a cozy winter's night.
>
> And when I hear this singing I stand dumbfounded, staggered, speechless that he is singing over me—one who has dishonored him so many times and in so many ways. It is almost too good to be true. He is rejoicing over my good with all his heart and with all his soul. He virtually breaks forth into song when he hits upon a new way to do me good. I would not dare say this on my own authority. Nor could I say it if I had not seen another foundation for his joy than my own righteousness. But I have it on the authority of the prophet Jeremiah.
>
> 39) I will give them one heart and one way, that they may fear me for ever, *for their own good* and the good of their children after

> them. 40) I will make with them an everlasting covenant, that *I will not turn away from doing good to them;* and I will put the fear of me in their hearts, that they may not turn from me. 41) *I will rejoice in doing them good,* and I will plant them in this land in faithfulness, *with all my heart and with all my soul* (Jeremiah 32:39–41).[5]

God's promise to the Old Testament Jews, Piper goes on to explain, includes present-day Christians. God delights in doing good for His people.

Is this a new concept for you? How does it make you feel? Would you be surprised to find this theme running through Scripture? Take a look at the following passages that express God's delight in doing us good: Deuteronomy 30:9; Psalms 84:11–12; 147:10–11; Isaiah 65:17–19; Zephaniah 3:17; Ephesians 2:7.

___

___

___

Do you think our definition of good and God's definition of good are always the same?

___

___

___

Does good always mean happy, uplifted, getting everything we want, the absence of pain?

___

___

___

How do you think God defines good? Here are some ideas to start with: Jeremiah 29:11; Matthew 7:7–11; John 10:11; James 1:17–18.

5. John Piper, *The Pleasures of God* (Portland, Oreg.: Multnomah Press, 1991), pp. 187–88.

How can adversity be a good thing?

Listen. Do you hear singing?

Living Insights STUDY TWO

Shoosh! Shoosh! That's what we heard the whole time we were touring the house. We loved the floor plan and the price; it was just what we needed. But the house sits on the corner of a busy street. We wondered if the endless hiss of traffic would keep us awake at night.

"Oh, no, you'll get used to it," the owner said. "After a week or so, you won't even know it's there." We were skeptical, since we heard the noise from every room in the house. But the neighbors on the opposite corner shared the owner's optimism.

So we moved in. And they were right. For the first few days, the noise was unusual, out of place. Then it seemed to disappear; it just blended into our world. Oh, we still notice the occasional clunkers, whose owners believe that driving without a muffler helps others appreciate what's under the hood. And the souped-up Harley "Hogs" still get our attention when they splatter decibels against the wall like mud. For the most part, though, we're unaware of the street noise.

Just as we tune out passing traffic, so we can let God get too familiar, can't we? He used to get our attention, like we used to hear the shoosh. But now, well, we're used to Him. He's there, but He doesn't bother us, and we don't bother Him. He has simply blended into the background.

What a shame. Maybe we should open the windows and hear Him pass by again.

Chapter 13

STRENGTHENING YOUR GRIP ON ATTITUDES

Philippians 2:1–8, 14; 4:4–8

Like a famished dog gnawing away the last trace of meat from a bone, the Nazis stripped Victor Frankl's life down to almost nothing. They took all his possessions, including his clothes and his wedding ring. They shaved his head. They stole his freedom. They robbed him of his family—mother, father, brother, wife all perished in the concentration camps. Only one sister survived.

Once a renowned psychiatrist, Frankl was reduced to being slave labor at the notorious death camp Auschwitz. Most of his existence was spent laying railway tracks and digging; one time he had to dig a tunnel for a water main—alone. All the while he was starved, deprived of proper sleep, shouted at, threatened, abused. The Nazis' dehumanization program missed no detail.

Frankl could have refused to cooperate, forfeiting his life, such as it was. He could have seethed in hate, plotting his revenge. He could have adopted his captors' view of himself, that of a subhuman wretch allowed the privilege (or curse) of life in return for serving the Reich. He could have given up and died in hopelessness.

But Frankl, humiliated and robbed of every external possession, realized the Nazis could never steal, shape, or dictate one thing: a person's attitude. In his book *Man's Search for Meaning*, he writes of those prisoners whose heroic choices shone through the darkness.

> We who lived in concentration camps can remember the men who walked through the huts comforting others, giving away their last piece of bread. They may have been few in number, but they offer sufficient proof that everything can be taken from a man but one thing: the last of the human freedoms—to choose one's attitude in any given set of circumstances, to choose one's own way.
>
> And there were always choices to make. Every day, every hour, offered the opportunity to make a decision, a decision which determined whether you would or would not submit to those powers which

> threatened to rob you of your very self, your inner freedom; which determined whether or not you would become the plaything of circumstance, renouncing freedom and dignity to become molded into the form of the typical inmate.[1]

Let's look at this "last of the human freedoms" so we can keep from being "molded into the form of the typical inmate" of this world.

Attitude: It's Up to You

Our attitude can have more influence than our past, our education, money, circumstances, appearance, skills, failures, successes, or how others treat us.

Though most of us will probably never find ourselves in a concentration camp, the borders of our comfort zones will be assaulted by the unexpected. Our hearts will be stripped and shaven by disappointment, failure, unmet expectations, illness, frustration, and broken relationships. We don't, however, have to allow any of these things to dictate our responses. If our minds are guided by the Word of God, we can respond with a godly attitude.

Take the Philippians, for example.[2] Judging from Paul's admonitions to that church, they had a tendency toward disunity (compare 1:27; 4:2–3). But instead of fighting one another, Paul encouraged them to reflect an attitude rooted in their relationship with Christ.

> If therefore there is any encouragement in Christ, if there is any consolation of love, if there is any fellowship of the Spirit, if any affection and compassion, make my joy complete by being of the same mind, maintaining the same love, united in spirit, intent on one purpose. (2:1–2)

If . . . if . . . if . . . if. These begin four conditional clauses in the Greek. Commentator Robert Lightner explains the significance of this structure.

1. Victor E. Frankl, *Man's Search for Meaning*, trans. Ilse Lasch (Boston, Mass.: Beacon Press, 1962), pp. 65–66.

2. For another example of attitude's triumph over adversity, visit Paul and Silas in jail in Acts 16:16–40.

> The "if" clauses, being translations of first-class conditions in Greek, speak of certainties. So in this passage "if" may be translated "since." Paul wrote here about realities, not questionable things. Paul appealed on the basis of (a) encouragement from being united with Christ . . . (b) comfort from His love . . . (c) fellowship with the Spirit . . . (d) tenderness and compassion.[3]

"Since you have all these things," says Paul, "you have what you need to exercise godly attitudes toward one another."

An Attitude of Unselfish Humility

What kinds of attitudes should a Christian cultivate? In verses 3 and 4, the apostle gets more specific.

> Do nothing from selfishness or empty conceit, but with humility of mind let each of you regard one another as more important than himself; do not merely look out for your own personal interests, but also for the interests of others.

Paul's first admonishment is to change from being self-centered to being others-centered. It's the kind of attitude Christ had when He came to earth to die for our sins.

> Have this attitude in yourselves which was also in Christ Jesus, who, although He existed in the form of God, did not regard equality with God a thing to be grasped, but emptied Himself, taking the form of a bond-servant, and being made in the likeness of men. And being found in appearance as a man, He humbled Himself by becoming obedient to the point of death, even death on a cross. (vv. 5–8)

That's not an easy attitude to adopt. But did you happen to notice that little word *mind* back in verse 3? It provides the key to carrying out the command. When it comes right down to it, Jesus chose to come down from heaven and live among us. His humility

3. Robert P. Lightner, "Philippians," in *The Bible Knowledge Commentary*, New Testament edition, ed. John F. Walvoord and Roy B. Zuck (Wheaton, Ill.: Scripture Press Publications, Victor Books, 1983), p. 653.

was an act of the will. And it's the same with us. We can't feel humble or act humble until we think humble. Our instincts clamor, "Look out for number one," but we don't have to listen to that voice. We can shape our attitudes—and then our actions—to serve others.

An Attitude of Positive Cooperation

Now take a look at verse 14.

> Do all things without grumbling or disputing.

Grumbling is displeasure expressed in murmuring.[4] Listen to the sound of the Greek word—*goggusmos*. Sounds like grumbling, doesn't it? You can hear it every day at work—*goggusmos*, *goggusmos*. You can hear it in your homes—*goggusmos*, *goggusmos*. You can even hear it among the church staff.

If you want to *goggusmos* your way through life, you'll find plenty of company. But you'll also be discouraged, depressed, and disappointed. Paul exhorts us to conduct our lives in a spirit of cooperation—seeking to build up one another with our speech instead of tearing each other down.

An Attitude of Genuine Joy

It's hard to grumble when you're rejoicing.

> Rejoice in the Lord always; again I will say, rejoice! Let your forbearing spirit be known to all men. The Lord is near. (4:4–5)

Paul's words carry a lot of weight when you think about who he's writing to. The Philippian Christians weren't exactly living a life of luxury. They had a lot more to worry about than beating the crowd to the Neiman Marcus cafeteria on Sunday afternoon. They were being persecuted, ostracized, even executed by the Jews as well as the Romans.

How then, could they be expected to rejoice? Notice Paul doesn't say, "Rejoice in your circumstances." He says, "Rejoice *in the Lord*." Our joy is rooted in a Person, not in circumstances. Paul's next words tell us how to rejoice in the Lord.

4. Walter Bauer, A *Greek-English Lexicon of the New Testament and Other Early Christian Literature*, 2d ed. Revised and augmented by F. Wilbur Gingrich and Frederick W. Danker, from Walter Bauer's 5th ed., 1957 (Chicago, Ill.: University of Chicago Press, 1979), p. 164.

> Be anxious for nothing, but in everything by prayer and supplication with thanksgiving let your requests be made known to God. And the peace of God, which surpasses all comprehension, shall guard your hearts and your minds in Christ Jesus. (vv. 6–7)

Prayer shifts the load from our shoulders to God's, making room for the peace only He can provide.

Aggressive and Passive Alternatives

When circumstances overwhelm us, we have a choice to make—to focus on God or to focus on our problems. When we look at the problems too long, we usually drift to either blame or self-pity.

Blame

When life doesn't go our way, we often become aggressive. We start looking for people to blame—ourselves, others, even God. But if we blame ourselves when we're not responsible, we bind ourselves to the past and imprison our self-esteem in the dungeon of self-flagellation. If we blame someone else, we risk poisoning our relationship with that person. If we blame God, we lash out against our single most important source of help. One psychologist puts it this way:

> Only one kind of counselee [is] relatively hopeless: that person who blames other people for his or her problems. If you can own the mess you're in, . . . there is hope for you and help available. As long as you blame others, you will be a victim for the rest of your life.[5]

Sometimes things just happen; there is no one to blame. And even if there is, harboring hate instead of offering forgiveness will do little to make things better.

Self-pity

"Nobody loves me, everybody hates me—I think I'll eat some worms." You might remember that little ditty from childhood. Perhaps

5. Carl Rogers, as quoted by Bruce Larson, in *There's a Lot More to Health Than Not Being Sick* (Waco, Tex.: Word Books, 1981), pp. 46–47.

you've even sung it when self-pity, the passive response to life's circumstances, sets in. Self-pity keeps us down. It makes us feel like the victim of an unfair world. It tells us that life, which could once be trusted, has turned on us. Our countenance droops with despair, and our hearts sink in helplessness.

Feelings of loneliness often stir up self-pity. We begin to believe the lie that nobody, especially God, cares. That our problem is unique. "No one could possibly understand what I've been through," we cry. In this way, self-pity distorts reality.

Are you divorced? You're surrounded by others who have been divorced—and have made it through. Have you failed? Welcome to the club; not one of us is perfect. Have you sinned? There's only One who hasn't—the Lord Jesus Christ Himself. And because we're related to Him, God forgives us and beckons us to move ahead with Him as our focus. We're often harder on ourselves than God is. Don't be sucked in by self-pity.

Food for the Right Attitude

Paul, in his typical style, never tells us to avoid something without giving us something to practice in its place. In Philippians 4:8, he provides six thoughts to dwell on that will squelch the voices of blame and self-pity and help us develop a godly attitude. "Finally, brethren," he says,

> whatever is true,
> whatever is honorable,
> whatever is right,
> whatever is pure,
> whatever is lovely,
> whatever is of good repute,

"If there is any excellence," Paul concludes, "and if anything worthy of praise, let your mind dwell on these things."

Some people might call this a denial of reality, just the power of positive, but unrealistic, thinking. Not so. Look what comes first on the list: whatever is *true*. God doesn't want us to live in a dreamworld, where we deny the existence of hardship and escape into fantasy. Rather, He wants our attitudes to be rooted in truth.

Whatever is *honorable*. To honor is "to worship, revere."[6] "Dwell

6. Archibald Thomas Robertson, *Word Pictures in the New Testament* (Grand Rapids, Mich.: Baker Book House, 1931), vol. 4, pp. 459–60.

on the things that are worthy of respect," Paul is saying. Not thoughts and images that are flippant, cheap, superficial, and shallow.

Whatever is *right*—whatever conforms to God's standards.[7] An attitude that reflects Christlikeness is one that conforms to the Word, not the world (see Rom. 12:2).

Whatever is *pure*. This "refers to what is wholesome, not mixed with moral impurity."[8] *Purity* isn't a synonym for *prudishness*. A high-necked dress or a pious smile does not a pure person make. Purity means that we have thoughts and actions that can hold up to the scrutiny of God.

Whatever is *lovely*. The best translation here is probably *winsome*.[9] Maybe we need to work on this one most of all. How pleasant are we to be around? How cheerful? How enjoyable?

Finally, dwell on the things that are of *good repute*. Literally, "of good report."[10] This is the opposite of a "that's-just-me-and-people-can-take-it-or-leave-it" attitude. People of good repute, though not living to please others, care about how they come across.

A Concluding Thought

Yes, we can control our attitudes. Why else would Solomon advise:

> Watch over your heart with all diligence,
> For from it flow the springs of life. (Prov. 4:23)

Think of your mind as a safe deposit box. Every day, we make attitude "deposits" into that box. It's not like a checking or savings account or a mutual fund. We don't gain interest or receive dividends. We can take out only what we put in.

So fill that box with godly attitudes—like joy, humility, encouragement, forgiveness, love—and guard them. Don't let anyone steal them and replace them with selfishness, discouragement, vengeance, or hatred. Hold on to the key.

You fill the box. You determine how you'll respond to life.

Some of us are sweating under the blazing lights of adversity. We feel stripped of all that matters and broken beyond hope. Our

7. Lightner, "Philippians," p. 664.

8. Lightner, "Philippians," p. 664.

9. Robertson, *Word Pictures*, p. 460.

10. Robertson, *Word Pictures*, p. 460.

only reality seems to be the pain we feel. But we don't have to give up. We still have our minds and our will. And no Reich on earth can touch those, if we belong to the heavenly kingdom.

Living Insights STUDY ONE

The destruction seemed heartless, a complete disregard for art and effort. I don't know who had created the sand castle, but whoever it was had put his or her heart and soul into it. It rose from the beach like a fortress, ornate spires and intimidating walls visible from quite a distance.

The creator had, for some reason, abandoned this masterpiece. A boy, about eight or nine, strolled stealthily up to the castle and glanced around like a hoodlum about to splatter paint on a national monument. He took a step back and—*thud*—planted his foot into one of the towers, sending it crashing into the sand from which it came. He obviously enjoyed it. *Thud!* Another spire. *Thud!* Then a wall. He stomped on the ruins in a kind of victory dance, until a heap of dirt lay where a glorious castle once stood.

The destroyer skipped down the beach, unaware of the lesson he had just taught me. No matter how beautiful and majestic, sand castles eventually become victims of neglect. Regardless of how many hours we spend scooping, slapping, and shaping, we eventually have to leave the beach to go home. And those ornate spires and high walls are left to the destructive whims of pounding waves and passing vandals.

Attitudes can be like sand castles. They seem strong enough, but left unattended on life's beach, they crumble when assaulted. That's why Paul told the Roman Christians to shape and strengthen their attitudes according to Scripture instead of adopting the world's flimsy thinking.

> Do not conform any longer to the pattern of this world, but be transformed by the renewing of your mind. Then you will be able to test and approve what God's will is—his good, pleasing and perfect will. (Rom. 12:2 NIV)

Scripture builds rock-solid attitudes. Submit yourself to the sculpting truth of God's Word, and your attitude castle, though it may take a beating, will never fall. Here are some supplies to help you fashion godly attitudes: Luke 10:30–37; Romans 12:9–21; Ephesians 4:31–5:2; Colossians 3:12–17.

Living Insights — STUDY TWO

Who's in control of your attitudes? You or your circumstances? Are you beginning to take on the negative disposition floating around your work environment, or are you positive in spite of it? Have you forgiven your friend for hurting your feelings, or are you waiting for an opportunity to pay him back? Do you think the best of your mate or children, or do you expect the worst? Are you defensive or cooperative? An encourager or discourager? Joyful or joyless?

Write down a few attitudes that are being shaped by your environment instead of the Word of God. For example:

impatience

Now, see what corrections Scripture offers for destructive attitudes. Pick one biblical "counterattitude," (e.g., patience for impatience), then, using a concordance or a topical Bible, look up a passage or two that presents the godly attitude. Work on it this week asking God to help you reflect His character more than your circumstances.

Chapter 14

STRENGTHENING YOUR GRIP ON EVANGELISM

Acts 8:26–39

Does sharing your faith rank right up there with root canals on your list of desired activities? Don't feel alone. It seems that most Christians would rather do anything than witness. Why? Well, for several reasons.

One is *ignorance*—we don't really know how to go about it. Another reason is *indifference*. We have other things to think about, and besides, plenty of evangelists out there can do the job better than we could. Third, we're *afraid*. Nobody likes being made a fool of or being asked questions they can't answer—especially by a stranger. And what if the response is hostile? The whole idea is just too intimidating. Also, many of us have an unpleasant memory of a *bad experience* when someone grabbed us by the collar and shoved the gospel down our throat. We remember that embarrassed, intruded-upon, pressured feeling, and the last thing we want to do is make someone else feel that way.

We've probably all been in situations—maybe on a plane, maybe at a convention—when the topic of religion came up and we had to face that inevitable dialogue with a nonbeliever. We've usually ended up feeling awkward and uncomfortable, and we've walked away wondering, What could I have done to not only win a hearing but keep a hearing? How could I have shown Christ to that person in a more understandable way? How could I have kept from sounding so pious or so out of touch with reality?

Good questions. And tucked away in Acts 8 is a series of answers. In this chapter is a story about a man named Philip. He was like most of us, but he was also a fervent evangelist. The principles we find in his life relate to every Christian.

This chapter has been adapted from "Discovering Your Part in Reaching the Lost," in the study guide *Making New Discoveries*, coauthored by Gary Matlack, from the Bible-teaching ministry of Charles R. Swindoll (Anaheim, Calif.: Insight for Living, 1995), pp. 50–55.

Philip's Background: From Persecution to Proclamation

In the first century, the seeds of the gospel were scattered by the winds of persecution. With Saul of Tarsus looking on, religious leaders stoned Stephen after his compelling—and convicting—sermon (Acts 7:52–60). Those stones sent ripples of persecution through Jerusalem, driving believers out to all of Judea and Samaria (8:1b). Did persecution dampen their spirits? No, just the opposite:

> Therefore, those who had been scattered went about preaching the word. (v. 4)

One of those scattered, preaching Christians was a man named Philip.

Philip's "Person-to-Person" Experience

Through Philip, God had stirred up the city of Samaria into a state of revival (8:5–13). When the apostles heard that he was up to his ears in new believers, they dispatched Peter and John to help him (vv. 14–25). How encouraging! Their ministry was burgeoning, and people were growing in the love of God. This would be a great place to settle down and nurture new believers, wouldn't it? Well, don't hammer down that tent peg so fast.

Right in the middle of this flourishing metropolitan ministry, the Lord uprooted Philip and set him on a desert road . . . to reach one person. Verses 26–39 record the experience, from which six key words emerge to help us share the gospel with people we encounter.

Sensitivity

> But an angel of the Lord spoke to Philip saying, "Arise and go south to the road that descends from Jerusalem to Gaza." (This is a desert road.) And he arose and went. (vv. 26–27a)

Oh, that we were all so sensitive to God's leading! Philip "arose and went" immediately after the angel directed him southward. No questions. No bargaining. No complaints about being pulled from city revival to wilderness witnessing. He just went.

What about us? Do we keep our spiritual sails unfurled, watching for them to flutter with a gust of God's wind? Or do we prefer to row along at our own speed, oblivious to the breeze? Through

Scripture, circumstances, and inner promptings, the Holy Spirit will guide us. But reaching others for Christ requires that we stay sensitive to His leading, whether we're on a plane, in a classroom, in the office, or sitting in our neighbor's living room.

Availability

> And behold, there was an Ethiopian eunuch, a court official of Candace, queen of the Ethiopians, who was in charge of all her treasure; and he had come to Jerusalem to worship. And he was returning and sitting in his chariot, and was reading the prophet Isaiah. And the Spirit said to Philip, "Go up and join this chariot." (vv. 27b–29)

Availability and sensitivity are twins—with slight variations. Both entail openness to God's leading; but where *sensitivity* emphasizes the ears (listening to and initially responding to God), *availability* focuses more on the feet (moving them in whatever direction God specifies). Sensitivity says, "I hear You, Lord, and I'm on my way." Availability says, "OK, where's the next turn?" Once Philip left Samaria, he kept his eyes open for God's road signs.

The Spirit led him to a royal eunuch poring over the Scriptures in his chariot. Commentator Simon Kistemaker describes this traveler as "the chief treasurer. He has the prominent position of chancellor of the exchequer, or finance minister, in charge of the royal treasury and national revenue" of Ethiopia.[1] William Barclay sheds light on the purpose of the man's journey:

> This eunuch had been to Jerusalem to worship. In those days the world was full of people who were weary of the many gods and the loose morals of the nations. They came to Judaism and there found the one God and the austere moral standards which gave life meaning. If they accepted Judaism and were circumcised they were called *proselytes*; if they did not go that length but continued to attend the Jewish synagogues and to read the Jewish scriptures they were called *God-fearers*. This Ethiopian must have

1. Simon J. Kistemaker, *New Testament Commentary: Exposition of the Acts of the Apostles* (Grand Rapids, Mich.: Baker Book House, 1990), p. 312.

> been one of these searchers who came to rest in Judaism either as a proselyte or a God-fearer.[2]

So Philip, taking his directions from the Spirit of God, pulled up beside this inquisitive official.

Initiative

As he approached the chariot, Philip heard the familiar words of Isaiah 53 read contemplatively by the Ethiopian. What do you think was going through the evangelist's mind just then? "Oh, this is too good to be true—he's reading about the Messiah. OK, deep breaths, deep breaths. I've got him now. Just another minute and . . ." Not likely, judging from the text:

> And when Philip had run up, he heard him reading Isaiah the prophet, and said, "Do you understand what you are reading?" (v. 30)

Philip started with a simple, yet thoughtful, question—and waited for an answer. He took the initiative in the conversation, setting a tone that didn't try to impress or insult. He just asked a question. There's nothing like a good question to open people up and introduce the topic of spirituality. You might want to try some of these:

- "What do you think is wrong with the world today?"
- "Who do you think is the greatest person who ever lived?"
- "You know, there's a lot about the 'religious right' in the news today. I'm curious, what's your perception of Christianity?"
- "Do you find in your line of work that most people are honest and treat others fairly?"

Just remember, taking the initiative doesn't mean we have to bully people with our message. Truth and tact can come bundled in the same package.

Tactfulness

The gospel of Christ isn't a box of chocolates. Not everyone

2. William Barclay, *The Acts of the Apostles*, rev. ed., The Daily Study Bible Series (Philadelphia, Pa.: Westminster Press, 1976), pp. 68–69.

who gets a taste will say, "What a treat. Can I have some more?" The message will offend many, simply because it makes clear distinctions between right and wrong (see Matt. 15:12; Rom. 9:33). We, however, don't have to add to the offense by *being offensive*. In fact, one of the most important principles we can remember is *to put ourselves in the other person's shoes*. If you remember nothing else, remember that. The Cross is to be offensive, not Christians (see 1 Cor. 1:18–25).

Philip treated the eunuch with respect, courtesy, and dignity. In answer to Philip's question, the eunuch responded:

> "Well, how could I, unless someone guides me?" And he invited Philip to come up and sit with him. Now the passage of Scripture which he was reading was this:
>
> "He was led as a sheep to slaughter;
And as a lamb before its shearer is silent,
So He does not open His mouth.
In humiliation His judgment was taken away;
Who shall relate His generation?
For His life is removed from the earth."
>
> And the eunuch answered Philip and said, "Please tell me, of whom does the prophet say this? Of himself, or of someone else?" (Acts 8:31–34)

Philip asked a question (v. 30) and waited for an answer. He listened. He was attentive. He waited to be invited into the chariot. And he lovingly led the eunuch through the pages of the Old Testament to Christ Himself (v. 35).

Our attitude and actions make a big difference in whether we're granted a hearing. Ironically, some Christians seem most un-Christlike when they're sharing His very words. We need to dispense with pushiness and pride and instead demonstrate Jesus' kindness and humility. Listen more. Judge less. Talk *with* people, not *at* them. Smile. Look the person in the eye. Offer a firm handshake.

By the way, there's nothing winsome about bad breath or body odor. The difference between repelling and attracting a non-Christian could be as simple as a breath mint or stick of deodorant.

Isn't it worth the effort to be tactful, courteous, and pleasant—considering how precious this unsaved person is to God?

Precision

Philip was not only courteous, he was also precise. That is, he kept the conversation focused on Christ.

> And Philip opened his mouth, and beginning from this Scripture he preached Jesus to him. (v. 35)

We think of preaching as speaking before a large crowd. Philip, however, "preached" to one person. Did he stand up, then, in the chariot and ask for a show of hands or deliver an altar call? No. The word for *preached* here can be translated simply "told him the good news" (NIV).

Starting with the eunuch's frame of reference, Isaiah 53, Philip shared the good news of Jesus Christ. He didn't debate various theories on when the book of Isaiah was written. He avoided bad-mouthing the synagogue for failing to declare Christ. He didn't present a survey of world religions. Nor did he condemn the eunuch for his employment in a pagan government. He simply shared Christ.

When we engage others in this kind of conversation, we need to understand that many are in the midst of inner distractions. Some may have been mistreated by Christians. Others are running from God, sending up smoke screens to avoid facing their predicament. Still others are downright antagonistic toward the faith. When such dynamics enter our discussions with nonbelievers, we must acknowledge their concerns but keep the spotlight on the death and resurrection of Jesus Christ.

Decisiveness

> And as they went along the road they came to some water; and the eunuch said, "Look! Water! What prevents me from being baptized?" And Philip said, "If you believe with all your heart, you may." And he answered and said, "I believe that Jesus Christ is the Son of God." And he ordered the chariot to stop; and they both went down into the water, Philip as well as the eunuch; and he baptized him. (Acts 8:36–38)

"Can I be baptized now?"

"Wait a minute," said Philip. "Do you believe what I've shared with you?"

Having presented the message, Philip helped the eunuch understand that following Christ involves making a clear decision.

A word of caution here. Some evangelism techniques emphasize "closing the sale." In other words, guiding people to the point of decision, getting them to pray the "sinner's prayer" before we leave them. But there are a couple of dangers in this kind of approach.

If we make a "prayer of salvation" our goal, we might be tempted to manipulate the message to that end—making the gospel something it's not. Such an approach can also cause us to stop viewing the lost as real people with real needs. Instead, they become "targets," potential notches on our Bible.

We need to realize that our responsibility is to clearly communicate the message, not convert sinners. It is the Holy Spirit who draws people to Christ and provides the gift of eternal life.

When God does lead individuals to embrace the gospel during a conversation, as He did with the eunuch, we can help them understand their decision and get them started on the road to new life. Which is what Philip did. And the eunuch "went on his way rejoicing" (v. 39b), carrying the seeds of the gospel home to Africa.

Closing Comments

Many evangelism-shy Christians say to themselves, "I can be a silent partner in winning the world to Christ. I'll simply live my faith instead of talking about it all the time."

It's true—when it comes to witnessing, few things are as important as living a godly life. But to say that's all it takes is like saying a plane needs only one wing to fly. As Paul observed,

> But how shall they ask [the Lord] to save them unless they believe in him? And how can they believe in him if they have never heard about him? And how can they hear about him unless someone tells them? (Rom. 10:14 TLB)

God has placed you where He has placed no one else. No one else in the world has the same relationships you have. No one will stand in the same grocery store line at exactly the same moment you do. No one else will come across a hungering diplomat in the desert at exactly the same time you do.

God hasn't put you in those places merely to model the truth. Listen for the voice of the Spirit to whisper in your ear. Watch for the stranger on the road. And be aware of your opportunities to go where He would send you.

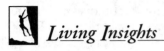

Living Insights STUDY ONE

Philip's encounter with the Ethiopian gives us a model to follow when sharing our faith. He was sensitive to the Lord's leading. He made himself available without reservation. He initiated a discussion of spiritual things. He was tactful. He kept the conversation focused on Christ. And he emphasized the need for decisiveness.

Believe it or not, though, Philip could have done all these things and still left out the primary element of any gospel presentation—the Scriptures. He could have, but he didn't. He knew that Isaiah 53 was a prophecy about Christ. So he used the very passage the Ethiopian was studying as an entry point to teach him about Jesus (Acts 8:35; see also Luke 24:27).

What good is the right method if we have the wrong message? Or an unclear message? Or one based on something besides what God has revealed in His Word? The Scriptures are central in our clear communication of the wonderful news of God's grace. We simply must know the Word if we are to reach the world.

If someone sat down beside you right now and asked you to show them what the Bible has to say about salvation in Christ, could you do it? What passages would you go to for information on God's holiness, our sinfulness, Christ's death on our behalf, His resurrection, our redemption, and the blessings of living the Christian life?

Why not take some time right now to put together a gospel presentation using some key passages. Then you'll be ready, as Peter says, "to make a defense to everyone who asks you to give an account for the hope that is in you, yet with gentleness and reverence" (1 Pet. 3:15). You might want to use some or all of the following passages.

Genesis 3:8–21
Isaiah 53
John 3:1–17
Acts 4:8–12
Romans 5:6–21
1 Corinthians 15:1–8
Galatians 2:16
Ephesians 2:1–10

Living Insights STUDY TWO

Is evangelism God's work or ours?

Well, it's both. Only God can save souls, and His Word opens hearts to His grace. But He includes us in the process; He wants us to communicate His message.

Some evangelism techniques, however, stress our part so much that we begin to believe that getting others saved is completely our responsibility. So if throngs of people don't accept our message, we feel guilty. We begin to keep score, comparing ourselves to those who are herding people into the kingdom. We're even tempted to tamper with the gospel—tone it down, pump it up, hang the world's bells and whistles on it—in order to elicit a positive response.

As if God had left us on our own!

If you wonder if you're really cut out to share the gospel, or if you're discouraged about a lack of "results" in your outreach ministry, you need to be refreshed by a timely reminder. God alone reaches into hearts and softens them. God is the only one who can change rebels into worshipers. It's God who forgives our sins and clothes us in Christ's righteousness, allowing us to stand before Him without fear of judgment.

We are responsible only for planting the seed of the gospel, with the care and attention of any good farmer. We don't control the condition of others' hearts, and we don't cause the growth (compare Luke 8:4–15; 1 Cor. 3:6–7).

Think of evangelism, then, not as working for God, but as participating in the work He is already doing. So the next time you talk to that coworker in your company or that neighbor in the front yard, remember—God's in charge. He's working behind the scenes according to His own time schedule. And His gospel message is never wasted, because it can't fail (see Isa. 55:10–11).

So share your faith. And leave the results to God.

Chapter 15

STRENGTHENING YOUR GRIP ON AUTHORITY

1 Samuel 15

I tell ya, I don't get no respect."

Comedian Rodney Dangerfield has built a career around that phrase. Daubing sweat from his forehead with a handkerchief and giving his necktie an occasional nervous jerk, he delivers a medley of one-liners until we roar with laughter at his pitiful lot in life. His wife doesn't pay attention to him. His kids tell him to go to his room. And his dog's favorite bone happens to be in his arm. Dangerfield has created a character with an authority crisis, a man whose dilemma is our delight.

A man whose dilemma, unfortunately, is also our dilemma. And if we didn't laugh so hard, we'd probably cry.

How many of you teachers spend the majority of your class time just trying to get your students under control? How many of you principals keep your eyes peeled, not just for students skipping class, but for kids carrying weapons or selling drugs? You police officers realize that, to many, your badge is no longer an emblem of honor and respect but a target to shoot at. And what about you bosses? Ever get the feeling that your employees would rather do anything other than what they're supposed to?

You parents also know all too well the frustration of having your authority undermined, not just by defiant and willful children but by their peers, other parents who are lax, the media, and extremist children's rights groups.

Granted, because many people abuse their positions of power, we need to question and challenge their authority. However, the problem lies not with authority itself, but with the specific people who corrupt it. Authority should serve and protect those under it.

Leaders, employers, teachers, and parents all have a right to be respected and obeyed. For as we learn to submit to their authority, we learn to submit to the greatest authority of all—God's.

Conversely, rebellion against earthly authority leads to rebellion against God, which is the most serious rebellion of all.

The Roots of Rebellion

All rebellion has its roots in our ancient parents, Adam and Eve. When they disobeyed God, the weeds of defiance invaded the Garden of Eden—and the entire human race (see Rom. 5:12), beginning with their first two children, one of whom committed the first murder in history.

You remember the story. Cain and Abel both brought sacrifices to the Lord. Abel brought the kind the Lord wanted him to bring; Cain brought the kind *he* wanted to bring. God accepted Abel's sacrifice, but He rejected Cain's. So Cain, enraged with envy, killed his brother (Gen. 4:3–8). And this, after the Lord had warned Cain to get a handle on his seething anger (vv. 6–7). After the deed, God confronted the rebel.

> Then the Lord said to Cain, "Where is Abel your brother?" And he said, "I do not know. Am I my brother's keeper?" (v. 9)

The Living Bible highlights the defiance in Cain's response: "How should I know? Am I supposed to keep track of him wherever he goes?" Cain not only disregarded God's wishes and sought to satisfy his lust for revenge, he dared to tell God that He had no right to question him! Cain's rebellion resulted in his brother's death and in banishment for himself. Refusing to obey God seems freeing for the moment, but it always has consequences.

Rebellion, however, doesn't always reveal itself in such a drastic way as Cain's murder of Abel. Sometimes it's more subtle; silently convincing our heart that the time has come to free ourselves from the "tyranny" of our heavenly Ruler—to live life our way instead of God's.

How Rebellion Reveals Itself

King Saul bears the infamous reputation of one who spurned the very God who had appointed him king of Israel. Where David was known as a man after God's own heart (1 Sam. 13:14; Acts 13:22), Saul could rightly be labeled a man after *Saul's* own heart. Just take a look at his track record of rebellion.

In 1 Samuel 13, Saul gets tired of waiting on the prophet Samuel and offers a sacrifice himself at Gilgal, showing impatient disregard for the priestly office (vv. 8–9). In chapter 14, he misuses the authority God has given him by making an impulsive vow that nearly cost his son's life (vv. 24–45).

In 1 Samuel 15, God seems to be giving Saul one more chance to submit to His authority. But the king rebels once again. In doing so, he shows us four primary ways that rebellion reveals itself.

Defying Authority to Fulfill Our Desires

As usual, God lays out His instructions with crystal clarity, conveying them through the prophet Samuel.

> Then Samuel said to Saul, "The Lord sent me to anoint you as king over His people, over Israel; now therefore, listen to the words of the Lord. Thus says the Lord of hosts, 'I will punish Amalek for what he did to Israel, how he set himself against him on the way while he was coming up from Egypt. Now go and strike Amalek and utterly destroy all that he has, and do not spare him; but put to death both man and woman, child and infant, ox and sheep, camel and donkey.'" (1 Sam. 15:1–3)

That's straightforward enough. It was payback time for the Amalekites, as commentator Eugene Merrill explains.

> Long before the time of Saul, in the days of the wilderness wandering, Israel had been savagely attacked from the rear by the Amalekites, a deed the Lord had promised to avenge someday (Ex. 17:8–16). The time had now come, so Samuel commanded Saul to destroy the Amalekites totally.[1]

So Saul jumps into action and carries out the Lord's command. Or does he?

> So Saul defeated the Amalekites, from Havilah as you go to Shur, which is east of Egypt. And he captured Agag the king of the Amalekites alive, and utterly destroyed all the people with the edge of the sword. But Saul and the people spared Agag and the best of the sheep, the oxen, the fatlings, the lambs,

1. Eugene H. Merrill, "1 Samuel," in *The Bible Knowledge Commentary*, Old Testament edition, ed. John F. Walvoord and Roy B. Zuck (Wheaton, Ill.: Scripture Press Publications, Victor Books, 1985), p. 447.

> and all that was good, and were not willing to destroy them utterly; but everything despised and worthless, that they utterly destroyed. (1 Sam. 15:7–9)

God had said, "Utterly destroy all" and "do not spare him." But Saul does spare Agag and some of the choice livestock. He was "not willing to destroy them utterly." Admittedly, he did *some* of what the Lord commanded. Which is the tricky part of detecting rebellion: it doesn't mean we *never* do anything God tells us to do; it means we fail to do *all* He tells us to do. Rebellion can be as simple as letting our own desires nudge ahead of the desire to obey Him fully.

Rationalization and Cover-up to Excuse Sinful Actions

The unenviable duty of confronting Saul's rebellion falls to Samuel, as usual, who grieves over the king's disobedience.

> Then the word of the Lord came to Samuel, saying, "I regret that I have made Saul king, for he has turned back from following Me, and has not carried out My commands." And Samuel was distressed and cried out to the Lord all night. (vv. 10–11)

By the time Samuel shows up to confront Saul, the king has convinced himself that he acted in accordance with God's command.

> And Samuel rose early in the morning to meet Saul; and it was told Samuel, saying, "Saul came to Carmel, and behold, he set up a monument for himself, then turned and proceeded on down to Gilgal." And Samuel came to Saul, and Saul said to him, "Blessed are you of the Lord! I have carried out the command of the Lord." (vv. 12–13)

Did you notice a slight discrepancy between Saul's assessment of his own actions and God's evaluation? Rebels are masters of twisting the truth to justify their behavior. In other words, they rationalize. The word *rationalize*, according to Webster, means "to attribute (one's actions) to rational and creditable motives without analysis of true and especially unconscious motives . . . to provide plausible but untrue reasons for conduct."[2]

2. *Merriam-Webster's Collegiate Dictionary*, 10th ed., see "rationalize."

We don't like to admit we're rebels; that's such a harsh word. We prefer euphemisms. So we try to soften our sin with phrases like these:

- "Hey, no big deal. God forgives, doesn't He?"
- "How else am I going to relate to the world?"
- "I'm only human."
- "Surely God didn't mean *that*—not for this culture, this age. Come on, we're coming up on the twenty-first century."
- "Well, at least I'm not as bad as old so-and-so."

Yes, God forgives. His grace covers all our sins, if we have trusted in Christ for our salvation. And, compared to others, we may not look so bad. But when we disobey God, He still calls it sin. That word needs to drift back into our vocabulary. When we confess our sins, instead of trying to cover them up, then we can run to Christ and stand in His cleansing light. But the more we rationalize, the more comfortable we become with rebellion, until we don't see the darkness of our sin anymore.

Defensiveness When Confronted with the Truth

Though Saul tries to disguise his disobedience, Samuel isn't fooled.

> But Samuel said, "What then is this bleating of the sheep in my ears, and the lowing of the oxen which I hear?" (v. 14)

Like a child caught sneaking cookies before dinner, Saul has his hand in the cookie jar and crumbs all over his face. Does the king own up to his sin? No way. Instead, he gets defensive and pins the blame on others.

> And Saul said, "They have brought them from the Amalekites, for the people spared the best of the sheep and oxen, to sacrifice to the Lord your God; but the rest we have utterly destroyed." (v. 15)

Can you feel the defensiveness in Saul's response, his shifting of the blame? "*They* have brought them," he says. "*The people* spared the best." "*The people* took some of the spoil" (see also v. 21). Only when things look good does he claim to have taken part: "But the rest *we* have utterly destroyed" (v. 15).

Remember Adam's response when God confronted him in the Garden of Eden? "It's this woman you gave me; it's her fault" (see Gen. 3:12). Saul tries the same tactic. And once again, it doesn't work.

Resistance to Accountability When Wrong Has Been Committed

By now Samuel has heard enough.

> Then Samuel said to Saul, "Wait, and let me tell you what the Lord said to me last night." And he said to him, "Speak!"
>
> And Samuel said, "Is it not true, though you were little in your own eyes, you were made the head of the tribes of Israel? And the Lord anointed you king over Israel, and the Lord sent you on a mission, and said, 'Go and utterly destroy the sinners, the Amalekites, and fight against them until they are exterminated.' Why then did you not obey the voice of the Lord, but rushed upon the spoil and did what was evil in the sight of the Lord?"
>
> Then Saul said to Samuel, "I did obey the voice of the Lord, and went on the mission on which the Lord sent me, and have brought back Agag the king of Amalek, and have utterly destroyed the Amalekites. But the people took some of the spoil, sheep and oxen, the choicest of the things devoted to destruction, to sacrifice to the Lord your God at Gilgal." (1 Sam. 15:16–21)

Worse than blatantly ignoring God's command, Saul reinterpreted it. He didn't want to be accountable to anyone but himself. So he marched into the city of Amalek with his own agenda. And he tries to make his rebellion sound so noble: "Better to sacrifice the animals to God than to merely destroy them."

Samuel, however, sees right through Saul's pious veneer.

> And Samuel said,
> "Has the Lord as much delight in burnt
> offering and sacrifices
> As in obeying the voice of the Lord?
> Behold, to obey is better than sacrifice,

And to heed than the fat of rams.
For rebellion is as the sin of divination,
And insubordination is as iniquity and
idolatry.[3]
Because you have rejected the word of the
Lord,
He has also rejected you from being king."
(vv. 22–23)

"Nice try, Saul, but you're forgetting one thing: that's not what God told you to do." God wants and deserves obedience. His instructions are always right and always for our good—even when they don't feel like it.

Epilogue to Rebellion

Finally, like an alcoholic no longer able to deny liquor's dominating control, Saul admits his sin.

> Then Saul said to Samuel, "I have sinned; I have indeed transgressed the command of the Lord and your words, because I feared the people and listened to their voice. Now therefore, please pardon my sin and return with me, that I may worship the Lord." (vv. 24–25)

But it's too late. Though he eventually goes back with Saul for appearance's sake (vv. 26–31), Samuel finishes the job the king was supposed to do—and never sees "Saul again until the day of his death" (vv. 32–33, 35). And God forever rejects Saul as king of Israel (vv. 28–29).

God forgives rebellion. In fact, the Bible tells us that, while we were still lost in our sins, Christ died for us (Rom. 5:8). But rebellion has consequences. For Saul, the price was his throne and his sanity. For us, it might be relationships, including our walk with God. It may be our ministry or our marriage. There's always a price.

3. Rebellion is like divination and insubordination is like idolatry in that each of them puts something besides God on the throne of our lives. Anything that takes the place of God's rightful authority—whether ourselves, a spirit, or an idol—is wrong. Authority belongs only to Him.

Applications to the Three Stages of Life

How, then, can we avoid rebelling against God's authority? Perhaps more than in any institution, the home is where respect for authority must be cultivated. Here are some suggestions for all three stages of life, beginning with children in the home.

Children

A *rebellious nature is conceived in a home where parents relinquish control.* Believe it or not, children don't want complete control. They think they do, but they can't handle it. They need the loving limits of guidelines and boundaries. That's why discipline is so important. Discipline tells children that their parents love them too much to let them rebel (see Prov. 13:24). So parents, model godly, loving authority, and your kids will be more likely to respect not only you but God as well.

Teens

A *rebellious spirit is cultivated among peers who resist control.* "Bad company corrupts good morals," as 1 Corinthians 15:33 says. Even children who respect authority will be tempted to hang around with rebellious peers. And among adolescents, peer pressure is a powerful influence. Parents, then, need to work hard at communicating. Remember the struggles you went through as a teen; then take a more empathetic interest in your children's lives during this time. Though it may not seem like it, they still need you.

Adults

A *rebellious life is crushed by God when He regains control.* We can't resist God's authority forever. At some point, perhaps later in life, He'll bring circumstances into our lives to teach us the importance of submission (see Prov. 29:1; 1:24–33). God sometimes has to rock the boat to get us back on course.

Living Insights STUDY ONE

Some people resist authority because they've had too much freedom—their parents rarely disciplined them; they almost always got what they wanted; they were seldom told no. Others, however, rebel because they were abused by those in authority over them.

They were beaten by parents, molested by a teacher or church leader, or submitted to regimentation—even legalism—that was heavy on rules and light on love.

Biblical authority is balanced authority. God's Word cautions those in charge to resist using their position as a license for abuse of any kind. "Overseers" in the church, for example, were never meant to ride roughshod over the congregation but to lovingly protect and guide them (Acts 20:28–35; 1 Pet. 5:1–4). Their spiritual qualities were to be impeccable (1 Tim. 3:1–7; Titus 1:5–9).

Husbands, though given the responsibility of spiritual leadership in the family, are instructed to exercise that leadership with sacrificial and others-centered love (Eph. 5:25–33). And parents are to apply discipline in a way that draws their children closer to the Lord, instead of driving them away from Him (Eph. 6:4; Col. 3:21).

Even Jesus Christ, who possesses all authority "in heaven and on earth" (Matt. 28:18), washed the feet of His disciples (John 13:1–15). And the Lord God, who has authority to do whatever He wants with His creation, has chosen to allow sinners to draw near Him through the grace provided in His Son (Heb. 4:14–16).

True authority is neither disinterested nor dictatorial. It is loving leadership.

How have you handled your authority? Have you ever abused it? Have you neglected it? What could you have done differently? What changes can you make in your life to restore biblical balance to your role as a parent, teacher, Christian leader, or employer?

Living Insights STUDY TWO

Have you ever been abused by someone in authority? How has that affected your view of God? Do you believe that He's abusive, that He wishes you harm?

What do the following passages tell you about God's authority?

Psalm 8

Psalm 112

Hebrews 12:5–13

Even though earthly authority falls short because of sin, God never abuses His authority. He can't; He's perfect.

Chapter 16

STRENGTHENING YOUR GRIP ON THE FAMILY

Psalms 127–128

What Is a Family? The title of Edith Schaeffer's book from twenty years ago asks an interesting question—one she answers in chapters with such titles as "The Birthplace of Creativity," "A Formation Center for Human Relationships," and "A Shelter in the Time of Storm."[1]

Today, however, a more accurate title for her book might be *What Should a Family Be?* Because, as we all know, many homes display more criticism than creativity, fracture more relationships than they foster, and contribute to life's storms instead of providing protection from them.

To strengthen our grip on what God intended for the family, let's turn to His Word, specifically Psalms 127 and 128. Though not a detailed manual for successful family life, these two ancient hymns paint a mural of inspired images that can help us appreciate, as well as improve, our families.

A Panoramic View

Imagine these two psalms as a sprawling portrait depicting four stages of family life: the foundation of the home (Ps. 127:1–2); the expansion of the home (vv. 3–5); the child-rearing years (Ps. 128:1–3); and the later years (vv. 4–6).

First Scene: The Foundational Years

Any home must rest on a firm foundation, both structurally and spiritually.

> Unless the Lord builds the house,
> They labor in vain who build it;
> Unless the Lord guards the city,
> The watchman keeps awake in vain. (Ps. 127:1)

1. Edith Schaeffer, *What Is a Family?* (Old Tappan, N.J.: Fleming H. Revell Co., Power Books, 1975).

What good is a home, even an elaborate one, if it's thrown together by an incompetent builder? Or what good does it do to hire a security guard if he can't hold off an intruder?

God is the Master Builder. His blueprint for living is infallible. His skill is unmatched; His materials, impenetrable. And if He guards the city and the home, who can overtake them? He's always alert, He never sleeps, and He can overpower any attacker.

In short, work done independently of God is futile. Unless a husband and wife build their home according to God's Word and entrust it to His care, their work and their watchfulness will be wasted. For the family to survive the wind, rain, theft, and vandalism of today's world, God must be the builder.

Some people, when they sense trouble in the family, try to strengthen the home by working longer hours and accumulating more material things. But, according to verse 2 of Psalm 127, that plan doesn't work.

> It is vain for you to rise up early,
> To retire late,
> To eat the bread of painful labors;
> For He gives to His beloved even in his sleep.

God isn't condemning work here; He created it (see Gen. 1:26–31; 2:15). Yet we need to realize that everything we have, even the blessings of a healthy home life, come from Him. The faithfulness of His hands, not the feverish frenzy of our own hands, secures our provision.

Second Scene: The Expansion Years

When children come along, everything changes, doesn't it? More mouths to feed, more bills to pay, more burdens to bear, and less time to enjoy life, right?

That's not quite how God looks at children. You'll never see Him describing kids as "rug rats," "interruptions," or "curtain-climbers." To Him, they're gifts, rewards, and a source of strength.

> Behold, children are a gift of the Lord. (Ps. 127:3a)

The Hebrew idea of *gift* goes beyond wrapped and ribboned birthday or Christmas presents. The word means "property" or "possession." Our children belong to God, and He has entrusted them to our care. As earthly stewards of these little ones, we have the joy and privilege of equipping them for life . . . and then releasing them to live it.

The psalmist follows this description with another image in the latter half of the verse:

> The fruit of the womb is a reward. (v. 3b)

Let's pause first on the phrase "fruit of the womb." Like growing apples in an orchard, child-rearing takes time, care, nurturing, and cultivation. The image suggests attention rather than neglect, interest rather than irritation. Luscious fruit doesn't suddenly appear on the limb. It's cultivated by a diligent farmer who tills, sows, waters, fertilizes, weeds, and prunes. The only things that grow well untended are weeds.

So just as the harvest is the farmer's reward, so children are the parents' reward. The word *reward* here signifies a gracious expression of God's favor on His people rather than something that's earned. Commentator A. F. Kirkpatrick explains:

> As He bestowed upon Israel the possession of Canaan (Ex. 15:17; Deut. 4:21), not as an hereditary right, but of His own free-will, in accordance with His promise, so of His free gift and grace does He bestow the blessing of numerous children.[2]

What a thought! Children are a crawling, walking, talking reminder of God's favor—a great prize from the greatest of Givers.

Children are gifts and rewards to be treasured, fruit to be cultivated . . . and arrows to be honed and launched.

> Like arrows in the hand of a warrior,
> So are the children of one's youth.
> How blessed is the man whose quiver is full of them;
> They shall not be ashamed,
> When they speak with their enemies in the gate.
> (Ps. 127:4–5)

Archery is a precise skill. It requires perception, concentration, practice, and a clear vision of the target. Good archers keep their arrows strong and sharp. Likewise, good parents carefully file and smooth their children and help them grow strong in the Lord.

Arrows, though, weren't made to rattle around in the quiver

2. A. F. Kirkpatrick, *The Book of Psalms* (1902; Grand Rapids, Mich.: Baker Book House, 1982), p. 753.

forever. After all the sharpening, strengthening, preparing, and aiming, an arrow must be released. If we have done our jobs well, they will fly straight and true. But don't be deceived. We don't become good parents overnight. Like archery, parenting is a skill. It deserves our time, our attention, and, most of all, our prayers.[3]

Third Scene: The Child-Rearing Years

Psalm 128 depicts another scene in the family mural.

> How blessed is everyone who fears the Lord,
> Who walks in His ways.
> When you shall eat of the fruit of your hands,
> You will be happy and it will be well with you.
> (vv. 1–2)

Interesting, isn't it? This psalm begins where Psalm 127 does—with the Lord. He is the source of all blessing. A healthy family life begins with Him. As commentator Allen Ross explains, "Laboring in anxious independence of God is vain (127:2), but working under God and in obedience to His ways is fruitful (cf. 1:3).[4]

Specifically, how is it fruitful?

> Your wife shall be like a fruitful vine,
> Within your house,
> Your children like olive plants
> Around your table. (128:3)

Once again, the psalmist uses agricultural imagery to depict the blessing of a growing, flourishing family. Notice, though, that each member of the family grows in different ways. A vine grows differently from an olive plant. So, fathers, take note. Your job isn't to make carbon copies of yourself but to help your wife and children grow in the way God designed them.

3. Some commentators broaden the archery imagery to include the idea of a son's protection or defense of the family. Willem A. VanGemeren, for example, says, "The psalmist uses a metaphor of war as he likens the children of one's youth to 'arrows' (v. 4). As the arrows protect the warrior, so the godly man need not be afraid, when blessed with sons." Addressing the image of the quiver, he continues, "A house full of children, born before one becomes old (cf. Gen. 37:3), is a protection against loneliness and abandonment in society." "Psalms," in *The Expositor's Bible Commentary*, ed. Frank E. Gaebelein (Grand Rapids, Mich.: Zondervan Publishing House, Academic and Professional Books, 1991), vol. 5, pp. 794–95.

4. Allen P. Ross, "Psalms," in *The Bible Knowledge Commentary*, Old Testament edition, ed. John F. Walvoord and Roy B. Zuck (Wheaton, Ill.: Scripture Press Publications, Victor Books, 1985), p. 885.

Fourth Scene: The Closing Years

What about the "empty nest" years? Does this psalm provide any encouragement for hanging on after the kids leave?

> Behold, for thus shall the man be blessed
> Who fears the Lord.
>
> The Lord bless you from Zion,
> And may you see the prosperity of Jerusalem all
> the days of your life.
> Indeed, may you see your *children's children*.
> Peace be upon Israel! (vv. 4–6, emphasis added)

An empty nest doesn't have to mean an empty life. God continues to bless, even after our children are gone. He blesses us personally as we continue to walk with Him (v. 4). He blesses us corporately as His people; in this case the inhabitants of Jerusalem remain the object of His affection (v. 5). And He blesses us generationally by allowing us to see our children blessed with children of their own (v. 6a).

What is a family? It's an institution built, guided, and blessed by God. And one that honors Him. But perhaps the more important question is, What is *your* family?

Living Insights STUDY ONE

Perhaps your family looks nothing like the mural in Psalms 127 and 128. Maybe memories of abuse still keep you from considering your father "family." Perhaps you're struggling through a separation or divorce. Maybe your kids have turned out more like crooked sticks than straight arrows—and they want nothing to do with you. Or perhaps God has never blessed you with children, or with a spouse for that matter. Does that mean you're not part of a family? Not at all. If you've trusted in Christ, you're never out of God's family, the church.

The church is where imperfect people, just like you and me, gather to hear what a perfect God says

> about living . . .
> about dealing with the past . . .
> about mending relational wounds . . .
> about starting over.

Regardless of how your earthly family has turned out, you'll always be part of God's eternal family.

By the way, in case you're not part of God's family, there's only one way to join. You have to be adopted into it. To do that, you must confess that, like all of us, you're a sinner, and that you're incapable of doing anything in your own strength to gain God's favor and spend eternity with Him. Then you must put your trust in Jesus Christ, believing that His death and resurrection alone can set you free from sin and make you acceptable to God. He'll adopt you into His family, not because of anything you have done, but because of the perfect life Christ lived while on earth. And when this life is over, you'll spend eternity with the Lord in heaven (see Rom. 3:23; 1 Cor. 15:3–11; Eph. 2:4–10; Titus 3:5).

If you decide to join God's family, write to us. We'd like to know who you are and welcome you.

Living Insights STUDY TWO

Congratulations! You've held on through sixteen chapters of *Strengthening Your Grip*. We hope you found some solid truth to hang on to. Which chapters or topics were most helpful to you?

Is there one particular topic you would like to study further or work on applying more in your own life?

What can you do over the next weeks and months to continue strengthening your grip on that subject?

Thanks for joining us. And remember, even though our spiritual grip slips from time to time, our heavenly Father never lets go of us (John 10:27–28).

Books for Probing Further

Want to get a tighter grip on some of the topics we covered in this study? We recommend that you reach for some of the following books. When you feel your spiritual fingers slipping off of life's rope, they'll cover your hands like gloves.

Strengthening Your Grip

Swindoll, Charles R. *Strengthening Your Grip*. Dallas, Tex.: Word Publishing, 1982.

Priorities

MacArthur, John, Jr. *The Ultimate Priority*. Chicago, Ill.: Moody Press, 1983.

Involvement

Getz, Gene A. *Sharpening the Focus of the Church*. Wheaton, Ill.: Scripture Press Publications, Victor Books, 1984.

Encouragement

Crabb, Lawrence J., Jr., and Dan B. Allender. *Encouragement: The Key to Caring*. Grand Rapids, Mich.: Zondervan Publishing House, Pyranee Books, 1984.

Swindoll, Charles R. *Encourage Me*. Portland, Oreg.: Multnomah Press, 1982.

Purity

Duin, Julia. *Purity Makes the Heart Grow Stronger: Sexuality and the Single Christian*. Ann Arbor, Mich.: Servant Publications, Vine Books, 1988.

Sproul, R. C. *The Holiness of God*. Wheaton, Ill.: Tyndale House Publishers, 1985.

Money

Blue, Ron. *Master Your Money: A Step-by-Step Plan for Financial Freedom*. Nashville, Tenn.: Thomas Nelson Publishers, 1986.

Getz, Gene A. *Real Prosperity: Biblical Principles of Material Possessions*. Chicago, Ill.: Moody Press, 1990.

Integrity

Engstrom, Ted W., with Robert C. Larson. *Integrity*. Waco, Tex.: Word Books Publisher, 1987.

Wiersbe, Warren W. *The Integrity Crisis*. Nashville, Tenn.: Thomas Nelson Publishers, Oliver Nelson, 1988.

Discipleship

Petersen, Jim. *Lifestyle Discipleship: The Challenge of Following Jesus in Today's World*. Colorado Springs, Colo.: NavPress, 1993.

Peterson, Eugene H. *A Long Obedience in the Same Direction: Discipleship in an Instant Society*. Downers Grove, Ill.: InterVarsity Press, 1980.

Aging

Stafford, Tim. *As Our Years Increase: Loving, Caring, Preparing: A Guide*. Grand Rapids, Mich.: Zondervan Publishing House, Pyranee Books, 1989.

Prayer

Foster, Richard J. *Prayer: Finding the Heart's True Home*. San Francisco, Calif.: HarperSanFrancisco, 1992.

Wiersbe, Warren W., comp. *Classic Sermons on Prayer*. Grand Rapids, Mich.: Kregel Publications, 1987.

Leisure

Minirth, Frank, Don Hawkins, Paul Meier, and Richard Flournoy. *How to Beat Burnout*. Chicago, Ill.: Moody Press, 1986.

Missions

Borthwick, Paul. *A Mind for Missions*. Colorado Springs, Colo.: NavPress, 1987.

Godliness

Packer, J. I. *Knowing God.* Downers Grove, Ill.: InterVarsity Press, 1973.

Piper, John. *Desiring God: Meditations of a Christian Hedonist.* Portland, Oreg.: Multnomah Press, 1986.

Stafford, Tim. *Knowing the Face of God.* Grand Rapids, Mich.: Zondervan Publishing House, 1986.

Attitudes

Jeffress, Robert. *Choose Your Attitudes, Change Your Life.* Wheaton, Ill.: Scripture Press Publications, Victor Books, 1992.

Evangelism

Aldrich, Joseph C. *Life-Style Evangelism: Crossing Traditional Boundaries to Reach the Unbelieving World.* Portland, Oreg.: Multnomah Press, 1981.

Campolo, Tony, and Gordon Aeschliman. *50 Ways You Can Share Your Faith.* Downers Grove, Ill.: InterVarsity Press, 1992.

Green, Michael. *Evangelism through the Local Church.* Nashville, Tenn.: Thomas Nelson Publishers, Oliver Nelson, 1992.

Authority

Thatcher, Martha. *The Freedom of Obedience.* Colorado Springs, Colo.: NavPress, 1986.

The Family

Sproul, R. C. *The Intimate Marriage.* Wheaton, Ill.: Tyndale House Publishers, 1975.

Some of these books may be out of print and available only through a library. For those currently available, please contact your local Christian bookstore. Books by Charles R. Swindoll may be obtained through Insight for Living. IFL also offers some books by other authors—please note the ordering information that follows and contact the office that serves you.

Ordering Information

Strengthening Your Grip

Cassette Tapes and Study Guide

This Bible study guide was designed to be used independently or in conjunction with the broadcast of Chuck Swindoll's taped messages which are listed below. If you would like to order cassette tapes or further copies of this study guide, please see the information given below and the order forms provided at the end of this guide.

		U.S.	Canada
SYG	**Study guide**	**$ 4.95 ea.**	$ 6.50 ea.
SYGCS	**Cassette series, includes all individual tapes, album cover, and one complimentary study guide**	**52.75**	61.75
SYG 1–8	**Individual cassettes, includes messages A and B**	**6.00 ea.**	7.48 ea.

The prices are subject to change without notice.

SYG 1-A: ***Strengthening Your Grip on Priorities***—1 Thessalonians 2:1–13
B: ***Strengthening Your Grip on Involvement***—Acts 2:42–47; Romans 12:9–16; 1 Corinthians 12:20–27

SYG 2-A: ***Strengthening Your Grip on Encouragement***—Hebrews 10:19–25
B: ***Strengthening Your Grip on Purity***—1 Thessalonians 4:1–5; Matthew 18:15–17

SYG 3-A: ***Strengthening Your Grip on Money***—1 Timothy 6:3–19
B: ***Strengthening Your Grip on Integrity***—Psalm 75:5–7; 78:70–72

SYG 4-A: ***Strengthening Your Grip on Discipleship***—Matthew 28:16–20; Mark 3:13–14; Luke 14:25–33
B: ***Strengthening Your Grip on Aging***—Psalm 90; Joshua 14:6–14

SYG 5-A: ***Strengthening Your Grip on Prayer***—Matthew 6:5–15; Philippians 4:1–9
B: ***Strengthening Your Grip on Leisure***—Genesis 1–3

SYG 6-A: ***Strengthening Your Grip on Missions***—Isaiah 6:1–12
B: ***Strengthening Your Grip on Godliness***—
1 Corinthians 10:1–13

SYG 7-A: ***Strengthening Your Grip on Attitudes***—Philippians 2:1–8, 14; 4:4–8
B: ***Strengthening Your Grip on Evangelism***—Acts 8:26–39

SYG 8-A: ***Strengthening Your Grip on Authority***—1 Samuel 15
B: ***Strengthening Your Grip on Family***—
Psalms 127–128

How to Order by Phone or FAX

(Credit card orders only)

United States: 1-800-772-8888 from 7:00 A.M. to 4:30 P.M., Pacific time, Monday through Friday
FAX (714) 575-5496 anytime, day or night

Canada: 1-800-663-7639, Vancouver residents call (604) 596-2910 from 8:00 A.M. to 5:00 P.M., Pacific time, Monday through Friday
FAX (604) 596-2975 anytime, day or night

Australia and the South Pacific: (03) 9-872-4606 or FAX (03) 9-874-8890 from 8:00 A.M. to 5:00 P.M., Monday through Friday

---

Other International Locations: call the Ordering Services Department in the United States at (714) 575-5000 during the hours listed above.

How to Order by Mail

United States

- Mail to: Processing Services Department
  Insight for Living
  Post Office Box 69000
  Anaheim, CA 92817-0900
- Sales tax: California residents add 7.25%.
- Shipping and handling charges must be added to each order. See chart on order form for amount.
- Payment: personal checks, money orders, credit cards (Visa, MasterCard, Discover Card, and American Express). No invoices or COD orders available.
- $10 fee for *any* returned check.

Canada

- Mail to: Insight for Living Ministries
  Post Office Box 2510
  Vancouver, BC V6B 3W7
- Sales tax: please add 7% GST. British Columbia residents also add 7% sales tax (on tapes or cassette series).
- Shipping and handling charges must be added to each order. See chart on order form for amount.
- Payment: personal cheques, money orders, credit cards (Visa, MasterCard). No invoices or COD orders available.
- Delivery: approximately four weeks.

Australia and the South Pacific

- Mail to: Insight for Living, Inc.
  GPO Box 2823 EE
  Melbourne, Victoria 3001, Australia
- Shipping: add 25% to the total order.
- Delivery: approximately four to six weeks.
- Payment: personal checks payable in Australian funds, international money orders, or credit cards (Visa, MasterCard, and BankCard).

Other International Locations

- Mail to: Processing Services Department
  Insight for Living
  Post Office Box 69000
  Anaheim, CA 92817-0900
- Shipping and delivery time: please see chart that follows.
- Payment: personal checks payable in U.S. funds, international money orders, or credit cards (Visa, MasterCard, and American Express).

Type of Shipping	*Postage Cost*	*Delivery*
Surface	10% of total order*	6 to 10 weeks
Airmail	25% of total order*	under 6 weeks

**Use U.S. price as a base.*

Our Guarantee

Your complete satisfaction is our top priority here at Insight for Living. If you're not completely satisfied with anything you order, please return it for full credit, a refund, or a replacement, as *you* prefer.

Insight for Living Catalog

The Insight for Living catalog features study guides, tapes, and books by a variety of Christian authors. To obtain a free copy, call us at the numbers listed above.

Order Form

United States, Australia, and Other International Locations

(Canadian residents please use order form on reverse side.)

SYGCS represents the entire *Strengthening Your Grip* series in a special album cover, while SYG 1–8 are the individual tapes included in the series. SYG represents this study guide, should you desire to order additional copies.

SYG	**Study guide**	**$ 4.95 ea.**
SYGCS	**Cassette series, includes all individual tapes, album cover, and one complimentary study guide**	**52.75**
SYG 1–8	**Individual cassettes, includes messages A and B**	**6.00 ea.**

Product Code	Product Description	Quantity	Unit Price	Total
			$	$
			Subtotal	
			California Residents—Sales Tax *Add 7.25% of subtotal.*	
			UPS ❑ First Class ❑ *Shipping and handling must be added. See chart for charges.*	
			Non-United States Residents *Australia add 25%. All other locations: U.S. price plus 10% surface postage or 25% airmail.*	
			Gift to Insight for Living *Tax-deductible in the United States.*	
			Total Amount Due *Please do not send cash.*	$

Amount of Order	*First Class*	*UPS*
$ 7.50 and under	1.00	4.00
$ 7.51 to 12.50	1.50	4.25
$12.51 to 25.00	3.50	4.50
$25.01 to 35.00	4.50	4.75
$35.01 to 60.00	5.50	5.25
$60.01 and over	6.50	5.75

Fed Ex and Fourth Class are also available. Please call for details.

Prices are subject to change without notice.

Payment by: ❑ Check or money order payable to Insight for Living ❑ Credit card

(Circle one): Visa MasterCard Discover Card American Express BankCard (In Australia)

Number ____________________

Expiration Date __________ Signature ____________________

We cannot process your credit card purchase without your signature.

Name ____________________

Address ____________________

City ____________________ State __________

Zip Code __________ Country ____________________

Telephone (   ) ____________________ Radio Station ____ ____ ____ ____

If questions arise concerning your order, we may need to contact you.

Mail this order form to the Processing Services Department at one of these addresses:

Insight for Living
Post Office Box 69000, Anaheim, CA 92817-0900

Insight for Living, Inc.
GPO Box 2823 EE, Melbourne, VIC 3001, Australia

Order Form
Canadian Residents

(Residents of the United States, Australia, and other international locations, please use order form on reverse side.)

SYGCS represents the entire *Strengthening Your Grip* series in a special album cover, while SYG 1–8 are the individual tapes included in the series. SYG represents this study guide, should you desire to order additional copies.

SYG	**Study guide**	**$ 6.50 ea.**
SYGCS	**Cassette series, includes all individual tapes, album cover, and one complimentary study guide**	**61.75**
SYG 1–8	**Individual cassettes, includes messages A and B**	**7.48 ea.**

Product Code	Product Description	Quantity	Unit Price	Total
			$	$
			Subtotal	
			Add 7% GST	
			British Columbia Residents *Add 7% sales tax on individual tapes or cassette series.*	
			Shipping *Shipping and handling must be added. See chart for charges.*	
			Gift to Insight for Living Ministries *Tax-deductible in Canada.*	
			Total Amount Due *Please do not send cash.*	$

Amount of Order	*Canada Post*
Orders to $10.00	2.00
$10.01 to 30.00	3.50
$30.01 to 50.00	5.00
$50.01 to 99.99	7.00
$100 and over	Free

Loomis is also available. Please call for details.

Prices are subject to change without notice.

Payment by: ❑ Cheque or money order payable to Insight for Living Ministries
❑ Credit card

(Circle one): Visa MasterCard Number ____________________

Expiration Date __________ Signature ____________________
We cannot process your credit card purchase without your signature.

Name ____________________

Address ____________________

City ____________________ Province __________

Postal Code __________ Country ____________________

Telephone (   ) ____________________ Radio Station ____ ____ ____ ____
If questions arise concerning your order, we may need to contact you.

Mail this order form to the Processing Services Department at the following address:

Insight for Living Ministries
Post Office Box 2510
Vancouver, BC, Canada V6B 3W7

CANADIAN COUNCIL OF CHRISTIAN CHARITIES · CCCC · FINANCIAL ACCOUNTABILITY

Order Form

United States, Australia, and Other International Locations

(Canadian residents please use order form on reverse side.)

SYGCS represents the entire *Strengthening Your Grip* series in a special album cover, while SYG 1–8 are the individual tapes included in the series. SYG represents this study guide, should you desire to order additional copies.

SYG	**Study guide**	**$ 4.95 ea.**
SYGCS	**Cassette series, includes all individual tapes, album cover, and one complimentary study guide**	**52.75**
SYG 1–8	**Individual cassettes, includes messages A and B**	**6.00 ea.**

Product Code	Product Description	Quantity	Unit Price	Total
			$	$

Subtotal	
California Residents—Sales Tax *Add 7.25% of subtotal.*	
UPS ❑ First Class ❑ *Shipping and handling must be added. See chart for charges.*	
Non-United States Residents *Australia add 25%. All other locations: U.S. price plus 10% surface postage or 25% airmail.*	
Gift to Insight for Living *Tax-deductible in the United States.*	
Total Amount Due *Please do not send cash.*	$

Amount of Order	*First Class*	*UPS*
$ 7.50 and under	1.00	4.00
$ 7.51 to 12.50	1.50	4.25
$12.51 to 25.00	3.50	4.50
$25.01 to 35.00	4.50	4.75
$35.01 to 60.00	5.50	5.25
$60.01 and over	6.50	5.75

Fed Ex and Fourth Class are also available. Please call for details.

Prices are subject to change without notice.

Payment by: ❑ Check or money order payable to Insight for Living ❑ Credit card

(Circle one): Visa MasterCard Discover Card American Express BankCard (In Australia)

Number ______________________________

Expiration Date __________ Signature ______________________________

We cannot process your credit card purchase without your signature.

Name ______________________________

Address ______________________________

City ______________________________ State __________

Zip Code __________ Country ______________________________

Telephone ( ) ______________ Radio Station ____ ____ ____ ____

If questions arise concerning your order, we may need to contact you.

Mail this order form to the Processing Services Department at one of these addresses:

Insight for Living
Post Office Box 69000, Anaheim, CA 92817-0900

Insight for Living, Inc.
GPO Box 2823 EE, Melbourne, VIC 3001, Australia

Order Form

Canadian Residents

(Residents of the United States, Australia, and other international locations, please use order form on reverse side.)

SYGCS represents the entire *Strengthening Your Grip* series in a special album cover, while SYG 1–8 are the individual tapes included in the series. SYG represents this study guide, should you desire to order additional copies.

SYG	**Study guide**	**$ 6.50 ea.**
SYGCS	**Cassette series, includes all individual tapes, album cover, and one complimentary study guide**	**61.75**
SYG 1–8	**Individual cassettes, includes messages A and B**	**7.48 ea.**

Product Code	Product Description	Quantity	Unit Price	Total
			$	$

Subtotal	
Add 7% GST	
British Columbia Residents *Add 7% sales tax on individual tapes or cassette series.*	
Shipping *Shipping and handling must be added. See chart for charges.*	
Gift to Insight for Living Ministries *Tax-deductible in Canada.*	
Total Amount Due *Please do not send cash.*	$

Amount of Order	*Canada Post*
Orders to $10.00	2.00
$10.01 to 30.00	3.50
$30.01 to 50.00	5.00
$50.01 to 99.99	7.00
$100 and over	Free

Loomis is also available. Please call for details.

Prices are subject to change without notice.

Payment by: ❑ Cheque or money order payable to Insight for Living Ministries
❑ Credit card

(Circle one): Visa MasterCard Number ____________________

Expiration Date __________ Signature ____________________
We cannot process your credit card purchase without your signature.

Name ____________________

Address ____________________

City ____________________ Province __________

Postal Code __________ Country ____________________

Telephone (   ) ____________________ Radio Station ____ ____ ____ ____
If questions arise concerning your order, we may need to contact you.

Mail this order form to the Processing Services Department at the following address:

Insight for Living Ministries
Post Office Box 2510
Vancouver, BC, Canada V6B 3W7